The Gulf War
did not
take place

The Gulf War did not take place

Jean Baudrillard

Translated and with an
introduction by
Paul Patton

INDIANA UNIVERSITY PRESS
BLOOMINGTON & INDIANAPOLIS

The Gulf War did not take place was originally published
in French as *La Guerre du Golfe n'a pas eu lieu.*
© 1991, Éditions Galilée

Manufactured in the United States of America

Library of Congress Cataloging-in-Publication Data

Baudrillard, Jean.
    [Guerre du Golfe n'a pas eu lieu. English]
    The Gulf War did not take place / Jean Baudrillard ;
translated and with an introduction by Paul Patton.
      p. cm.
    Includes bibliographical references (p.).
    ISBN 0-253-32946-9 (alk. paper). — ISBN 0-253-21003-8
(pbk. : alk. paper)
    1. Persian Gulf War, 1991—Miscellanea. 2. Persian Gulf War,
1991—Press coverage—Miscellanea. I. Title.
DS79.72.B3813 1995
956.7044'2—dc20   95-19574

  2 3 4 5 00 99 98 97 96

Contents

The Gulf War
did not
take place

Introduction

Jean Baudrillard's article, "The Gulf War will not take place,"
was published in *Libération* on 4 January 1991, a little over one
month after the UN Security Council had voted to authorise the
use of force if Iraq had not begun to remove its troops from
Kuwait by January 15, and a little under two weeks before the
American and British air attack on Baghdad and Iraqi positions
in Kuwait. Far from being deterred by the unfolding situation,
he wrote two more pieces along similar lines: "The Gulf War: is
it really taking place?" which referred to the events during
February 1991, and "The Gulf War did not take place," which
was written after the end of hostilities on 28 February. Part of
the second article appeared in *Libération* on 6 February while a
fragment of the third article appeared in *Libération* on 29
March 1991. All three pieces first appeared in extended form in
the book published in May 1991.[1]

The central thesis of Baudrillard's essays appears to be directly contradicted by the facts. What took place during January
and February 1991 was a massive aerial bombardment of Iraq's
military and civil infrastructure. According to some accounts,
the amount of high explosive unleashed in the first month of the
conflict exceeded that of the entire allied air offensive during

WW II.[2] This was followed by a systematic air and land assault on the Iraqi forces left in Kuwait, which culminated in the infamous "turkey shoot" carried out on the troops and others fleeing along the road to Basra. Official estimates of lives lost as direct casualties of these attacks are in the order of 100,000, but these do not take into account the subsequent loss of life due to hunger and disease. On the face of it, Baudrillard could not have been more wrong. So why did he pursue this line of argument which appears to deny the reality of the Gulf War?

At the time, the TV Gulf War must have seemed to many viewers a perfect Baudrillardian simulacrum, a hyperreal scenario in which events lose their identity and signifiers fade into one another. Fascination and horror at the reality which seemed to unfold before our very eyes mingled with a pervasive sense of unreality as we recognised the elements of Hollywood script which had preceded the real (the John Wayne language and bearing of the military spokesmen), and as the signifiers of past events faded into those of the present (the oil-soaked sea bird recycled from the *Exxon Valdez* to warn of impending eco-disaster in the Gulf). Occasionally, the absurdity of the media's self-representation as purveyor of reality and immediacy broke through, in moments such as those when the CNN cameras crossed live to a group of reporters assembled somewhere in the Gulf, only to have them confess that they were also sitting around watching CNN in order to find out what was happening. Television news coverage appeared to have finally caught up with the logic of simulation.

It was not the first time that images of war had appeared on TV screens, but it was the first time that they were relayed "live" from the battlefront. It was not the first occasion on which the military censored what could be reported, but it did involve a new level of military control of reportage and images. Military planners had clearly learnt a great deal since Vietnam: procedures for controlling the media were developed and tested in the Falklands, Grenada and Panama. As a result, what we saw was for the most part a "clean" war, with lots of pictures of weaponry, including the amazing footage from the nose-cameras of "smart bombs," and relatively few images of human casualties, none from the Allied forces. In the words of one commentator, for the first time, "the power to create a crisis merges with the power to direct the movie about it ... Desert Storm was the first major global media crisis orchestration that made instant history."[3] The Gulf War movie was instant history in the sense that the selected images which were broadcast worldwide provoked immediate responses and then became frozen into the accepted story of the war: high-tech weapons, ecological disaster, the liberation of Kuwait. In case anyone missed the first release, CNN produced its own edited documentary, "CNN: War in the Gulf" which was shown on TV around the world. Within weeks of the end of hostilities, Time Warner produced a CD-ROM disk on Desert Storm which included published text, unedited correspondents' reports, photos and maps in the form of a single hypertext document. In their publicity, they described this interactive multimedia disk as a "first draft of history."

In "The Precession of Simulacra" Baudrillard took as an

allegory of simulation the Borges story in which the cartographers of an empire draw up a map so detailed that it exactly covers the territory.[4] Thanks to the geographical data collected by the US Defense Mapping Agency, remote corners of the American Empire such as Kuwait already exist on hard disk. Just as it marked a new level of military control over the public representation of combat operations, so the Gulf War displayed a new level of military deployment of simulation technology. Technological simulacra neither displace nor deter the violent reality of war, they have become an integral part of its operational procedures. Virtual environments are now incorporated into operational warplanes, filtering the real scene and presenting aircrew with a more readable world.[5] The development of flight simulators provided an early example of the computer technology which allowed the boundaries between simulation and reality to become blurred: the images and information which furnish the material for exercises and war games become indistinguishable from what would be encountered in a real conflict. The same technology now allows the creation of simulated environments in which to train tank crews, and even the possibility of connected simulators in which virtual tank battles can be fought out. An article in the first issue of *Wired* recounts developments in the use of networked simulation machines as training devices. Current research aims to achieve what is called "seamless manipulation" in which "the seams between reality and virtuality will be deliberately blurred" and "real tanks can engage simulator crews on real terrain which is simultaneously virtual." Within months of the end of the war, army historians and simulation modelers had produced their own multimedia, fully interactive, network capable digital simulation of one of the tank battles from the closing stages of the conflict: "armchair strategists can now fly over the virtual battlefield in the 'stealth vehicle,' the so-called 'SIMNET flying carpet,' viewing the 3-D virtual landscape from any angle during any moment of the battle. They can even change the parameters — give the Iraqis infrared targeting scopes, for instance, which they lacked at the time ... this is virtual reality as a new way of knowledge: a new and terrible kind of transcendent military power."[6]

Baudrillard at times portrays the Gulf conflict as one between a relentless and pre-programmed military machine and a hysterical trickster, a rug salesman whose essential weapons include the ruse and the decoy. (65–6) Quite apart from the orientalist overtones of this image, it underestimates the role played by dissimulation and deception operations within Allied military strategy. Electronic warfare involves new forms of deception by means of electronic interference and falsified signals. In the Gulf, such technological dissimulation was combined with old-fashioned tactical deception manoeuvres on the ground, with apparent success. American agents even succeeded in introducing a computer virus into Iraq's air defence command and control system.[7] Seen in this light, the use of the media to pass disinformation to the other side is simply another dimension of a consistent strategic embrace of the logic of simulation. The Gulf War thus witnessed the birth of a new kind of military apparatus which incorporates the power to control the production and circulation of images as well as the power to direct the actions of bodies and machines. It involved a new kind of event and a new kind of power which is at once both real and simulacral.

Baudrillard's essays pursue a high-risk writing strategy, courting equally the dangers of contradiction by the facts and self-refutation. They occasionally force the facts to fit their own rhetorical oppositions: for example, in claiming that "no accidents occurred in this war, everything unfolding according to programmatic order." (73) They rail against the proliferation of useless commentaries, yet do not hesitate to offer commentary of their own: for example, suggesting that there are more tricks to the wily Arab opponent than the Pentagon strategists suspect. (81) This is Baudrillard as armchair strategist and expert in the stratagems of symbolic exchange. They denounce the emptiness of the media event but also seek to endow it with the status of being an exemplary non-event. But these are not scholarly analyses of the events themselves, nor even of their media representation. Baudrillard is reluctant to claim the status of philosophy, sociology or political analysis for his writing, but equally resistant to its dismissal as literature or poetry. In time and with a little imagination, he has since suggested, it will be possible to read *The Gulf War did not take place* as if it were a science fiction novel.[8] These are occasional essays by a writer who believes that writing should be less a representation of reality than its transfiguration and that it should pursue a "fatal strategy" of pushing things to extremes. They are also immediate responses to instant history TV and its first draft versions in the print media. As such, they belong in the series of his essays which includes a discussion of the staged massacre at Timisoara, and the equally provocatively titled response to a television link-up with Sarajevo, "No Pity for Sarajevo."[9] The timing of their composition is important.

"The Gulf War will not take place" was written in December 1990 and January 1991, when the final act of the Gulf crisis was still to be played out. At one level, the response expressed in this article is a kind of *fuite en avant*, a sardonic challenge to the media hype surrounding the Gulf crisis. The point being made is that the events which were unfolding did not and would not correspond to what Baudrillard called the "archaic imaginary of media hysteria."(56) This imaginary object of media speculation was total war in the 1940s sense, including the use of chemical and perhaps even nuclear weapons. War in that sense did not take place, even though massive damage was inflicted by means of conventional weapons. Baudrillard's response to the subsequent events pursues the symbolic challenge to the manner in which these were portrayed. It is not irony so much as the kind of black humour which seeks to sub- vert what is being said by pursuing its implicit logic to extremes: so you want us to believe that this was a clean, minimalist war, with little collateral damage and few Allied casualties. Why stop there: war? what war?

Rhetoric aside, Baudrillard's first essay is also a response to the question which remained open at the time: will there or will there not be war? His answer points to an irony in events themselves which derives from the fact that war itself has become virtual. The hypothesis of "The Gulf War will not take place" is that the deterrence of war in the traditional sense has been internalised and turned back upon the Western powers, producing a form of self-deterrence which renders them incapable of realising their own power in the form of relations of force. Under present conditions, Baudrillard argues, the virtual has overtaken the actual, it functions to deter the real event and leaves only the simulacrum of war which will never advance to the use of force: "we are no longer in a logic of the passage from virtual to actual but in a hyperrealist logic of the deterrence of the real by the virtual."(27)

The underlying argument of this initial essay is that the logic of deterrence has transformed the nature of war. Deterrence is a matter of the virtual exercise of power, action upon the action of the other by immaterial means. It is a means of waging war, but one in which the aim is precisely non-engagement or the avoidance of direct encounter between the parties involved. The Cold War was indeed a war, one that has been fought and won, but increasingly by economic, informational and electronic means. It was a war fought on the principle of deterrence, on the basis of an economic, R&D and informational effort to deter any use of material force by the other side. It was won when the Soviet economic and political system could no longer maintain the effort. In the process, Baudrillard suggests, war evolved in a manner parallel to the evolution of capital: "just as wealth is no longer measured by the ostentation of wealth but by the secret circulation of speculative capital, so war is not measured by being unleashed but by its speculative unfolding in an abstract, electronic and informational space, the same one in which capital moves."(56) This does not mean that it is unreal in the sense of not having real effects, any more than a capital crisis is unreal because it takes place in the electronic and informational space of digitalised and networked financial markets. Rather, it means that state-of-the-art military power is now virtual in the sense that it is deployed in an abstract, electronic and informational space, and in the sense that its primary mechanism is no longer the use of force. Virtual war is therefore not simply the image or imaginary representation of real war, but a qualitatively different kind of war, the effects of which include the suppression of war in the old sense.

Shortly after the publication of "The Gulf War will not take place" the bombing began in earnest. At the end of that essay, Baudrillard offers a reason for undertaking what he calls the "stupid gamble" of attempting to demonstrate the impossibility of war in the Gulf just at the moment when all the signs were pointing in the direction of its occurrence, namely the stupidity of not doing so.(28) The stupidity in question is that of those critics who uncritically participate in the supposed realism of the information industry, or the stupidity of taking a position for or against the war without first interrogating the nature and type of reality proper to events such as those which unfolded in the Gulf and on our TV screens. For Baudrillard, in these essays, "it is not a question of being for or against the war. It is a question of being for or against *the reality of the war*. Analysis must not be sacrificed to the expression of anger. It must be entirely directed against reality, against the evidence; here, against the evidence of this war."[10]

Accordingly, a primary concern of the second essay, "The Gulf War: is it really taking place?", is to interrogate the nature of the Gulf War as a media event. This is not a war but a simulacrum of war, a virtual event which is less the representation of real war than a spectacle which serves a variety of political and strategic purposes on all sides. Here, the sense in which Baudrillard speaks of events as virtual is related to the idea that real events lose their identity when they attain the velocity of real time information, or to employ another metaphor, when they become encrusted with the information which represents them. In this sense, while televisual information claims to provide immediate access to real events, in fact what it does is produce informational events which stand in for the real, and which "inform" public opinion which in turn affects the course of subsequent events, both real and informational. As consumers of mass media, we never experience the bare material event but only the informational coating which renders it "sticky and unintelligible" like the oil-soaked sea bird.(32) Where was this image captured and what oil spill caused it? Who caused the oil spill to begin with? To the extent that real events are mediated and portrayed by such selected images, they become contaminated by what Baudrillard calls "the structural unreality of images."(46–7) The result is a new kind of entity, qualitatively different to "real" or "imaginary" events as these were understood prior to the advent of modern communications technology: virtual media events. These are informational entities and one of their defining characteristics is to be always open to interpretation. Informational events are thus the objects of endless speculation: because a range of interpretations is always possible, the identity of such events becomes vague or undecidable. Baudrillard's Gulf War essays provide many examples of such aporia: for example, throughout much of its duration, the war is both a non-event, an empty war in the sense that there is a lack of real engagement between the combatants, and an excessive, superabundant war in terms of the quantity of personnel and material involved.(33–4) On the one hand, the American decision-makers are unable to perceive the Other in any terms but their own, and as a result they misrecognise the strategic aims of Saddam Hussein; on the other, Hussein is entirely a mercenary beholden to outside forces and it is the West which is in conflict with itself in Iraq.(37–8) Finally, the Iraqi invasion of Kuwait may be represented as the outcome of the megalomaniac ambitions of a local dictator, or as the result of a deliberate ploy on the part of the American administration in order to legitimise its projection of force into the region.(71–2)

The images of war nonetheless have real effects and become enmeshed in the ensuing material and social reality. In this sense, Baudrillard argues, we live in a hyperreality which results from the fusion of the virtual and the real into a third order of reality. Much has been written since the Gulf crisis about the role of the media in promoting the military option, and about the practice of misinformation, lies and propaganda on both sides. There is no doubt that such things occurred. One of the more effective propaganda stories about Iraqi atrocities in Kuwait was the eye-witness account, before a Congressional Human Rights Caucus, of Iraqi soldiers removing babies from incubators and leaving them to die. It later emerged that the witness was the daughter of the Kuwaiti ambassador to the US, and that she had been coached by a public relations firm hired by the Kuwaiti Government.[11] On the other side, television footage of an outraged woman amid the rubble of an Iraqi neighbourhood was later shown to have featured an Assistant Deputy Foreign Minister and former ambassador to the US.[12] For some critics, such manipulation constitutes an abuse of the democratic right to information. However, the danger of a critical response which is confined to the denunciation of such abuses is that this also sustains what Baudrillard calls a "hypocritical vision of television and information."(46) It judges the media by reference to a moral ideal, namely that of a good or truthful use of images and signs. In fact, there is nothing inherently good about images or signs, and they can just as readily be employed to deceive as to tell the truth. As Baudrillard argues in his article on Timisoara, the indignant attempt to maintain a moral defence against the principle of simulation which governs all forms of representation misses the point: "the image and information are subject to no principle of truth or reality."[13] In this sense, it is cynics such as Saddam Hussein and the US military commanders who are less naive and hypocritical in their willingness to control information and images in whatever ways best serve their strategic ends: "We believe that they immorally pervert images. Not so. They alone are conscious of the profound immorality of images..."(47)

Informational events such as the Gulf crisis are endemic to postmodern public life. Since they are by definition always open to interpretation, they may be made to serve a variety of political ends. They are an important vector of power. What matters is to control the production and meaning of information in a given context. In effect, at least two strategies are in play with regard to the control of information in contemporary public life. During the "live" phase of a significant event such as the Gulf conflict or an election campaign, the strictest control of information is necessary in order to influence future developments. Wherever public opinion can feed back into a political process which includes the event in question, image and interpretation or "spin" upon current developments is vital. That is why the Gulf War movie was also an influential part of history even as it unfolded. Reports before and during the conflict phase directly influenced public opinion in support of the war. Film coverage of the bombing of retreating Iraqi forces was fundamental to the decision to end the war, since it was feared that such images would adversely affect public sentiment. The images of destruction and death along the road to Basra did not fit the script of the world's first high-tech clean war. Where enemy forces are reliant upon TV news for information, as it is argued the Iraqis were during the Gulf conflict, it becomes possible to employ the media directly as a conduit for disinformation. During the preparations for the land offensive, media reports of US Marines along the Saudi border with Kuwait and on amphibious ships off the coast were part of a calculated and successful strategy to deceive Iraqi commanders about the likely direction of the assault.[14] Reports of such deliberate deception imply that the use of media reports as part of the Allied military's operational conduct of the war was more extensive than even Baudrillard suggests.

However, once the live phase of the event is passed, another strategy takes over. The proliferation of archival information including taped audio-visual records allows the event to become utterly dispersed into a morass of conflicting interpretations and hypotheses about what really happened. Did Saddam Hussein undertake the invasion of Kuwait against all indications or was he lured into a trap by US policy makers? Who was really responsible for the assassination of JFK? And who killed Laura Palmer? It is this latter effect of the proliferation of information which sets limits to the effectiveness of the kind of critical media analysis which seeks to discover the truth of events. The author of *The Persian Gulf TV War*, Douglas Kellner, recounts his herculean efforts to obtain and cross-check information about the Gulf War. Despite this, his book opens with an admission of failure: he cannot decide conclusively for or against the conspiracy theory according to which the US enticed Iraq to invade Kuwait since "other accounts are also plausible."[15] It is the desire to avoid this kind of informational aporia which lies behind Baudrillard's injunction: "Resist the probability of any image or information whatever. Be more virtual than the events themselves, do not seek to re-establish the truth, we do not have the means, but do not be duped, and to that end re-immerse the war and all information in the virtuality from whence they came ... Be meteorologically sensitive to stupidity."(66–7) Not only does the real vanish into the virtual through an excess of information, it leaves an archival deposit such that "generations of video-zombies ... will never cease reconstituting the event."(47)

And even if we did possess the means to establish the truth, what difference would this make? For every book exposing the lies and inhumanity of US policy in the Gulf there are two more which champion it as the defence of democracy and the New World Order.

Christopher Norris regards Baudrillard's Gulf War essays as a definitive exposure of the intellectual and political bankruptcy of postmodern thought and a demonstration of "the depth of ideological *complicity* that exists between such forms of extreme anti-realist or irrationalist doctrine and the crisis of moral and political nerve" which afflicts Western intellectuals. According to Norris, Baudrillard's "absurd theses" about the war readily accord with "a 'postmodern' mood of widespread cynical acquiescence" and represent a form of "theory" which is "ill-equipped to mount any kind of effective critical resistance."[16] Claims of ideological complicity are notoriously difficult to prove or disprove, but there is little in Baudrillard's essays to suggest acquiescence in either the political and military operations carried out in the Gulf or their portrayal by the media. Indeed, the tone and argument of Baudrillard's essays is entirely directed against the complicity which results from the failure to question the reality and the nature of these events. Norris' own rhetorical stance is one which suggests that alternative theoretical approaches offer the prospect of "effective critical resistance." Yet Baudrillard at least published polemical pieces which addressed the political and media reality at the time. Norris seized the occasion to renew his campaign against the whole "postmodern tendency" in contemporary theory.

His argument largely repeats that of his earlier article on

Baudrillard and the politics of postmodernism.[17] On the one hand, he concedes the descriptive value of Baudrillard's account, allowing that "this is indeed in some sense a 'postmodern' war, an exercise in mass-manipulative rhetoric and 'hyperreal' suasive techniques, which does undoubtedly confirm some of Baudrillard's more canny diagnostic observations."[18] On the other, he rejects the epistemological scepticism which he takes to lie behind this postmodern tendency, and questions the supposed connection between the diagnosis of the postmodern condition and this philosophical conclusion. The flaw which runs through all postmodernist thinking is a confused epistemological argument which begins by denying that we have any means of access to "what happens" other than what is provided by the media, and ends by concluding on this basis that there is no "operative difference between truth and falsehood, veridical knowledge and its semblance."[19]

Understood in this manner, the thesis that the Gulf War did not take place would indeed be ludicrous, and would hardly justify the effort of a lengthy essay in reply. But epistemological scepticism founded upon the logic of representation is not part of Baudrillard's argument: not only does he make truth-claims about what happened, his interrogation of the reality of the media Gulf War presupposes that this is a different kind of event from those which occurred in the desert, a simulacrum rather than a distorted or misleading representation. These essays advance no universal claims about the collapse of the real into its forms of representation, but rather make specific ontological claims about aspects of present social reality, such as the virtual war which results from the strategy of deterrence and the virtual informational war which we experience through the media. At one point, it is true, Baudrillard reminds us that the direct transmission by CNN of information in real time does not prove that war is taking place.(61) However, his claim that the Gulf War did not take place does not depend upon the possibility of such technological fraud. Rather, it relies upon the two distinct notions of virtual war involved in deterrence and media simulation, and upon questioning whether the military operations undertaken by the Allies really constituted a war in the traditional sense. Useful criticism would engage with these notions rather than, as Norris does, attack a soft target of the critic's own invention.

Does the refusal of the critical strategy which seeks to re-establish the truth of what happened commit Baudrillard to the irrationalist denial that any military engagement took place? Alternatively, does the fact of military conflict constitute a refutation of the hypothesis that there was no Gulf War? It does only if we accept that what did take place out there in the desert beyond the reach of the TV cameras was in fact a war. Baudrillard's argument in "The Gulf War did not take place" is not that nothing took place, but rather that what took place was not a war. In the past, war has always involved an antagonistic and destructive confrontation between adversaries, a dual relation between warring parties. In several respects, this was not the case in the Gulf conflict. The disparity between US and Iraqi forces with regard to method and military technology was so great that direct engagement rarely took place, and when it did the outcome was entirely predictable. Whereas Iraq was disposed to fight in the manner of its previous war with Iran, and prepared to tolerate the massive casualties which would result from a ground-based war of attrition, the US and its allies sought a rapid conflict based upon airpower, high-technology intelligence and weapons systems, and the extensive use of electronic warfare. The almost complete absence of any engagement by Iraqi planes, and the fate of their technologically inferior tanks, testify to the one-sided nature of the conflict: "it is as though the Iraqis were electrocuted, lobotomised, running towards the television journalists in order to surrender or immobilised beside their tanks ... can this be called a war?" (67–8)

In his defence of the rationalist outlook which rejects the postmodern reduction of truth to consensus belief, Norris points to the figure of Chomsky as someone who is both a defender of Enlightenment ideals in morality and the philosophy of language, and a staunch critic of US foreign policy, a model of the liberal and critical intellectual. Yet Chomsky has also questioned whether what took place in the Gulf in 1990-1 was a war. He writes: "As I understand the concept 'war', it involves two sides in combat, say, shooting at each other. That did not happen in the Gulf."[20] He goes on to describe the successive phases of the conflict as involving varieties of state terrorism practised on both sides, and a form of slaughter practised by US and UK air and ground forces upon Iraqi soldiers and civilians. Other commentators have argued that the disparity between the aims, methods and military technology of the two sides was so great that what occurred cannot be considered an adversarial encounter. The imbalance of military means was such that this was not a conflict in which the survival of both sides was in play, but an entirely asymmetrical operation, an exercise in domination rather than an act of war. The claim that war itself has become virtual does not mean that military conflicts do not occur: they do and with increasing frequency and savagery in the New World Order. But these are secondary phenomena, like the persistence of sweatshops alongside fully automated production facilities. They are the consequences of a law of uneven development, located for the most part in a political and military third world. Where they do involve first world powers such as the US or UK, it is because they are in conflict with third world forces who do not recognise that the rules of the game have changed, or who, like Saddam Hussein, operate according to different rules. They are police operations rather than wars. In these cases, deterrence breaks down for lack of any common ground, and it is this failure of communication which leads to the use of force. However, the use of force remains carefully circumscribed, a lever of last resort employed only to the extent that is necessary to bring the recalcitrant party into line. The crucial stake in the Gulf affair, Baudrillard argues, was the subordination of Islam to the global order: "Our wars thus have less to do with the confrontation of warriors than with the domestication of the refractory forces on the planet ... All that is singular and irreducible must be reduced and absorbed. This is the law of democracy and the New World Order." (86)

This is not war, and even if it were, in the case of the Gulf conflict, it is as though it never happened. The final irony of the whole episode is that, apart from the massive damage and suffering inflicted upon Iraq, and the short-lived political and economic benefits at home, very little changed as a result of the military conflict. The Iraqi regime was allowed to remain intact, and its army permitted to crush the Kurdish and Shiite rebellions. The rights of Kuwait may have been restored, but in exchange for the rights of minorities in Iraq. The image of a just war fought between the forces of freedom and those of tyranny dissolved in the moral ambiguities of the post-conflict period. The same Americans who had systematically destroyed Iraq's power grid and transport infrastructure now refused to enforce the law of democracy and the New World Order where this would entail intervening in the internal affairs of a sovereign state. From a political point of view, it was no longer clear what had been gained by the sacrifice of so many lives. A perfect semblance of victory for the Americans was exchanged for the perfect semblance of defeat for Iraq.(71) In short, the Gulf War did not take place.

Several people answered my queries, discussed the text and read drafts of this translation. In addition to Jean Baudrillard, I would like to thank Rex Butler, Alan Cholodenko, Michael McKinley and Larbi Sadiki for their valuable assistance. I am especially grateful to Julian Pefanis and José Borghino for their careful checking and editing of the translation.

Notes

1   Jean Baudrillard, *La Guerre du Golfe n'a pas eu lieu*, Paris: Éditions Galilée, 1991. All subsequent references to this text in the Introduction refer to the translation which follows.

2   George Gerbner, "Persian Gulf War, the Movie" in *Triumph of the Image: The Media's War in the Persian Gulf — A Global Perspective*, edited by H. Mowlana, G. Gerbner and H.I. Schiller, Boulder and Oxford: Westview Press, 1992, p.252.

3   Gerbner, pp.244, 247.

4   Baudrillard, *Selected Writings*, ed Mark Poster, Cambridge: Polity Press, 1988, p.166.

5   Michael Heim, *The Metaphysics of Virtual Reality*, New York, Oxford: Oxford University Press, 1993, p.113.

6   Bruce Sterling, "War is Virtual Hell", *Wired* (1), 1993, pp.95-6.

7   Lieutenant-Colonel Jeffrey D. McCausland, *Adelphi Paper 282*, London: The International Institute for Strategic Studies, 1993, p.29.

8   *Baudrillard Live: Selected Interviews*, ed Mike Gane, London and New York, Routledge, pp.180-1, 203.

9   "Les charniers de Timisoara", in J. Baudrillard, *L'Illusion de la fin ou la grève des événements*, Paris: Editions Galilée, 1993; "Pas de pitié pour Sarajevo", *Libération*, 7 January 1994.

10   Baudrillard, *L'illusion de la fin*, p.95.

11   Douglas Kellner, *The Persian Gulf TV War*, Boulder: Westview Press, 1992, pp.67–8.

12   McCausland, *Adelphi Paper 282*, p.32.

13   Baudrillard, *L'illusion de la fin*, p.90.

14   William J. Taylor Jr and James Blackwell, "The Ground War in the Gulf", *Survival*, vol. XXXIII, no.3, May/June 1991, p.234.

15   Kellner, *The Persian Gulf TV War*, pp.7, 13.

16   Christopher Norris, *Uncritical Theory: Postmodernism, Intellectuals and the Gulf War*, London: Lawrence and Wishart, 1992, pp.27, 29.

17   Norris, "Lost in the Funhouse: Baudrillard and the politics of postmodernism", in *What's Wrong With Postmodernism*, Hemel Hempstead: Harvester Wheatsheaf, 1990, pp.164-93.

18   Norris, *Uncritical Theory* pp.25-6.

19   Norris, *Uncritical Theory* p.12.

20   Noam Chomsky, "The Media and the War: What War?", in *Triumph of the Image: The Media's War in the Persian Gulf — A Global Perspective*, edited by H. Mowlana, G. Gerbner and H.I. Schiller, p.51.

The Gulf War
will not take place

From the beginning, we knew that this war would never happen. After the hot war (the violence of conflict), after the cold war (the balance of terror), here comes the dead war — the unfrozen cold war — which leaves us to grapple with the corpse of war and the necessity of dealing with this decomposing corpse which nobody from the Gulf has managed to revive. America, Saddam Hussein and the Gulf powers are fighting over the corpse of war.

War has entered into a definitive crisis. It is too late for the (hot) WW III: this has already taken place, distilled down the years into the Cold War. There will be no other. It might have been supposed that the defection of the Eastern Bloc would have opened up new spaces of freedom for war by unlocking deterrence. Nothing of the sort, since deterrence has not come to an end, on the contrary. In the past it functioned as reciprocal deterrence between the two blocs on the basis of a virtual excess of the means of destruction. Today it functions all the

more effectively as self-deterrence, total self-deterrence up to
and including the self-dissolution of the Eastern Bloc, the profound self-deterrence of American power and of Western power
in general, paralysed by its own strength and incapable of
assuming it in the form of relations of force.

This is why the Gulf War will not take place. It is neither
reassuring nor comforting that it has become bogged in interminable suspense. In this sense, the gravity of the non-event in
the Gulf is even greater than the event of war: it corresponds to
the highly toxic period which affects a rotting corpse and which
can cause nausea and powerless stupor. Here again, our symbolic defences are weak: the mastery of the end of war escapes
us and we live all this in a uniform shameful indifference, just
like the hostages.

Non-war is characterised by that degenerate form of war
which includes hostage manipulation and negotiation.
Hostages and blackmail are the purest products of deterrence.
The hostage has taken the place of the warrior. He has become
the principal actor, the simulacral protagonist, or rather, in his
pure inaction, the protagoniser of non-war. The warriors bury
themselves in the desert leaving only hostages to occupy the
stage, including all of us as information hostages on the world
media stage. The hostage is the phantom actor, the extra who
occupies the powerless stage of war. Today, it is the hostage at
the strategic site, tomorrow the hostage as Christmas present,
as exchange value and liquidity. Fantastic degradation of that
which was the very figure of impossible exchange. With
Saddam Hussein, even that strong value has weakened and
become the symbol of weak war. Saddam has made himself the

capitalist of hostage value; after the market in slaves and prole-
tarians, the vulgar merchant of the hostage market. Taking the
place of the warrior's challenge, hostage value has become syn-
onymous with the debility of war. We are all hostages of media
intoxication, induced to believe in the war just as we were once
led to believe in the revolution in Romania, and confined to the
simulacrum of war as though confined to quarters. We are
already all strategic hostages *in situ*; our site is the screen on
which we are virtually bombarded day by day, even while serving as exchange value. In this sense, the grotesque vaudeville
played by Saddam Hussein is a diversion, at once a diversion of
both war and international terrorism. His soft terrorism will at
least have put an end to the hard terrorism of Palestinians and
others, thereby showing him to be in this as in many other
respects the perfect accomplice of the West.

This impossibility of proceeding to the act, this absence of
strategy, implies the triumph of blackmail as strategy (in the
case of Iran, there was still a challenge; with Saddam there is
only blackmail). Saddam Hussein's abjection lies in his having
vulgarised everything: religious challenge has become fake
holy war, the sacrificial hostage a commercial hostage, the violent refusal of the West a nationalistic scam and war an impossible comedy. But we have helped him to do this. By allowing
him to believe that he had won the war against Iran, we drove
him towards the mirage of a victory against the West — this
mercenary's revolt is indeed the only ironic and pleasing trait
of this whole story.

We are in neither a logic of war nor a logic of peace but in a logic of deterrence which has wound its way inexorably through forty years of cold war to a denouement in our current events; a logic of weak events, to which belong those in Eastern Europe as well as the Gulf War. Peripeteias of an anorexic history or an anorexic war which can no longer devour the enemy because it is incapable of conceiving the enemy as worthy of being challenged or annihilated — and God knows Saddam Hussein is worthy of neither challenge nor annihilation — and thus devours itself. It is the de-intensified state of war, that of the right to war under the green light of the UN and with an abundance of precautions and concessions. It is the bellicose equivalent of safe sex: make war like love with a condom! On the Richter scale, the Gulf War would not even reach two or three. The build-up is unreal, as though the fiction of an earthquake were created by manipulating the measuring instruments. It is neither the strong form nor the degree zero of war, but the weak or phthisical degree, the asymptotic form which allows a brush with war but no encounter, the transparent degree which allows war to be seen from the depths of the darkroom.

We should have been suspicious about the disappearance of the declaration of war, the disappearance of the symbolic passage to the act, which already presaged the disappearance of the end of hostilities, then of the distinction between winners and losers (the winner readily becomes the hostage of the loser: the Stockholm syndrome), then of operations themselves. Since it never began, this war is therefore interminable. By dint of dreaming of pure war, of an orbital war purged of all local and political peripeteias, we have fallen into soft war, into the virtual impossibility of war which translates into the paltry fantasia where adversaries compete in de-escalation, as though the irruption or the event of war had become obscene and insupportable, no longer sustainable, like every real event moreover. Everything is therefore transposed into the virtual, and we are confronted with a virtual apocalypse, a hegemony ultimately much more dangerous than real apocalypse.

The most widespread belief is in a logical progression from virtual to actual, according to which no available weapon will not one day be used and such a concentration of force cannot but lead to conflict. However, this is an Aristotelian logic which is no longer our own. Our virtual has definitively over-taken the actual and we must be content with this extreme virtuality which, unlike the Aristotelian, deters any passage to action. We are no longer in a logic of the passage from virtual to actual but in a hyperrealist logic of the deterrence of the real by the virtual.

In this process, the hostages are once again revealing. Extracted like molecules in an experimental process, then dis-tilled one by one in the exchange, it is their virtual death that is at issue, not their real death. Moreover, they never die: at best they disappear. There will never be a monument to the unknown hostage, everyone is too ashamed of him: the collec-tive shame which attaches to the hostage reflects the absolute degradation of real hostility (war) into virtual hospitality (Saddam Hussein's "guests").

The passage to action suffers widespread infamy: it suppos-edly corresponds to a brutal lifting of repression, thus to a psy-

chotic process. It seems that this obsession with the passage to
action today governs all our behaviour: obsession with every
real, with every real event, with every real violence, with every
pleasure which is too real. Against this obsession with the real
we have created a gigantic apparatus of simulation which
allows us to pass to the act "in vitro" (this is true even of pro-
creation). We prefer the exile of the virtual, of which television
is the universal mirror, to the catastrophe of the real.

War has not escaped this virtualisation which is like a surgical operation, the aim of which is to present a face-lifted war,
the cosmetically treated spectre of its death, and its even more
deceptive televisual subterfuge (as we saw at Timisoara). Even
the military has lost the privilege of use value, the privilege of
real war. Deterrence has passed by that way and it spares no-
one. No more than the politicians, the military personnel do
not know what to make of their real function, their function of
death and destruction. They are pledged to the decoy of war as
the others are to the decoy of power.

PS To demonstrate the impossibility of war just at the moment
when it must take place, when the signs of its occurrence are
accumulating, is a stupid gamble. But it would have been even
more stupid not to seize the opportunity.

The Gulf War:
is it really taking place?

We may well ask. On the available evidence (absence of images
and profusion of commentary), we could suppose an immense
promotional exercise like that one which once advertised a
brand-name (GARAP) whose product never became known.
Pure promotion which enjoyed an immense success because it
belonged to pure speculation.

The war is also pure and speculative, to the extent that we
do not see the real event that it could be or that it would signify.
It reminds us of that recent suspense advertisement: today I
take off the top, tomorrow I take off the bottom; today I unleash
virtual war, tomorrow I unleash real war. In the background, a
third advertisement in which an avaricious and lubricious
banker says: your money appeals to me. This sadly celebrated
advertisement is reincarnated by Saddam Hussein saying to the
West: your power appeals to me (as they rushed to palm off a
good share of it to him); then to the Arabs, with the same
hypocrisy: your religious war appeals to me (as they rushed to

put all their money on him).

In this manner, the war makes its way by promotion and speculation, including the use of hostages transformed into marketing ploys, and in the absence of any clarification of plans, balance sheets, losses or operations. No enterprise would survive such uncertainty, except precisely speculative risk management, otherwise known as the strategy of turning a profit from the worst, in other words, war (= Highly Profitable Senseless Project or HPSP). War itself has taken this speculative turn: it is highly profitable but uncertain. It can collapse from one day to the next.

Nevertheless, from this point onwards the promotional advantages are fabulous. Defeated or not, Saddam is assured of an unforgettable and charismatic label. Victorious or not, American armaments will have acquired an unequalled technological label. And the sumptuary expenditure in material is already equivalent to that of a real war, even if it has not taken place.

We have still not left the virtual war, in other words a sophisticated although often laughable build-up against the backdrop of a global indeterminacy of will to make war, even in Saddam's case. Hence the absence of images — which is neither accidental nor due to censorship but to the impossibility of illustrating this indeterminacy of the war.

Promotional, speculative, virtual: this war no longer corresponds to Clausewitz's formula of politics pursued by other means, it rather amounts to *the absence of politics pursued by other means*. Non-war is a terrible test of the status and the uncertainty of politics, just as a stock market crash (the speculative universe) is a crucial test of the economy and of the uncertainty of economic aims, just as any event whatever is a terrible test of the uncertainty and the aims of information. Thus "real time" information loses itself in a completely unreal space, finally furnishing the images of pure, useless, instantaneous television where its primordial function irrupts, namely that of filling a vacuum, blocking up the screen hole through which escapes the substance of events.

Nor is promotion the pursuit of the economy by other means. On the contrary, it is the pure product of uncertainty with regard to the rational aims of production. This is why it has become a relentless function, the emptiness of which fills our screens to the extent of the absence of any economic finality or rationality. This is why it competes victoriously with the war on our screens, both alternating in the same virtual credit of the image.

The media promote the war, the war promotes the media, and advertising competes with the war. Promotion is the most thick-skinned parasite in our culture. It would undoubtedly survive a nuclear conflict. It is our Last Judgement. But it is also like a biological function: it devours our substance, but it also allows us to metabolise what we absorb, like a parasitic plant or intestinal flora, it allows us to turn the world and the violence of the world into a consumable substance. So, war or promotion?

The war, along with the fake and presumptive warriors, generals, experts and television presenters we see speculating about it all through the day, watches itself in a mirror: am I pretty enough, am I operational enough, am I spectacular enough, am I sophisticated enough to make an entry onto the historical stage? Of course, this anxious interrogation increases the uncertainty with respect to its possible irruption. And this uncertainty invades our screens like a real oil slick, in the image of that blind sea bird stranded on a beach in the Gulf, which will remain the symbol-image of what we all are in front of our screens, in front of that sticky and unintelligible event.

Unlike earlier wars, in which there were political aims either of conquest or domination, what is at stake in this one is war itself: its status, its meaning, its future. It is beholden not to have an objective but to prove its very existence (this crisis of identity affects the existence of us all). In effect, it has lost much of its credibility. Who, apart from the Arab masses, is still capable of believing in it and becoming inflamed by it? Nevertheless, the spectacular drive of war remains intact. In the absence of the (greatly diminished) will to power, and the (problematic) will to knowledge, there remains today the widespread will to spectacle, and with it the obstinate desire to preserve its spectre or fiction (this is the fate of religions: they are no longer believed, but the disincarnate practice remains). Can war still be saved?

Certainly, Iran and Iraq did as much as they could to save the fiction of murderous, fratricidal, sacrificial and interminable (1914 style) war. But they were savages and that war from another period proved nothing with regard to the status and the possibility of a modern war. WW III did not take place and yet we are already beyond it, as though in the utopian space of a post-war-which-did-not-take-place, and it is in the suspense created by this non-place that the present confrontations unfold and the question is posed: can a war still take place?

This one is perhaps only a test, a desperate attempt to see whether war is still possible.

Empty war: it brings to mind those games in World Cup football which often had to be decided by penalties (sorry spectacle), because of the impossibility of forcing a decision. As though the players punished themselves by means of "penalties" for not having been able to play and take the match in full battle. We might as well have begun with the penalties and dispensed with the game and its sterile stand-off. So with the war: it could have begun at the end and spared us the forced spectacle of this unreal war where nothing is extreme and which, whatever the outcome, will leave behind the smell of undigested programming, and the entire world irritated as though after an unsuccessful copulation.

It is a war of excesses (of means, of material, etc.), a war of shedding or purging stocks, of experimental deployment, of liquidation and firesale, along with the display of future ranges of weaponry. A war between excessive, superabundant and over-equipped societies (Iraq included), committed both to waste (including human waste) and the necessity of getting rid of it.

Just as the waste of time nourishes the hell of leisure, so technological wastes nourish the hell of war. Wastes which incarnate
the secret violence of this society, uncoerced and non-degrad-
able defecation. The renowned American stocks of WW II sur-
plus, which appeared to us as luxury, have become a suffocating global burden, and war functions well within its possibilities in this role of purgative and expenditure.

If the critical intellectual is in the process of disappearing, it
seems by contrast that his phobia of the real and of action has
been distilled throughout the sanguineous and cerebral network of our institutions. In this sense, the entire world including the military is caught up in a process of intellectualisation.

See them become confused in explanations, outdo themselves in justifications and lose themselves in technical details
(war drifts slowly into technological mannerism) or in the
deontology of a pure electronic war without hitches: these are
aesthetes speaking, postponing settlement dates into the
interminable and decisions into the undecidable. Their war-
processors, their radars, their lasers and their screens render
the passage to war as futile and impossible as the use of a
word-processor renders futile and impossible the passage to
the act of writing, because it removes from it in advance any
dramatic uncertainty.

The generals also exhaust their artificial intelligence in cor-
recting their scenario, polishing their war script so much that
they sometimes make errors of manipulation and lose the plot.
The famous philosophical épochè has become universal, on the

screens as much as on the field of battle.

Should we applaud the fact that all these techniques of war-processing culminate in the elision of the duration and the violence of war? Only eventually, for the indefinite delay of the war is itself heavy with deadly consequences in all domains.

By virtue of having been anticipated in all its details and exhausted by all the scenarios, this war ends up resembling the hero of *Italien des Roses* (Richard Bohringer in the film by Charles Matton), who hesitates to dive from the top of a building for an hour and a half, before a crowd at first hanging on his movements, then disappointed and overcome by the suspense, exactly as we are today by the media blackmail and the illusion of war. It is as though it had taken place ten times already: why would we want it to take place again? It is the same in *Italien des Roses* : we know that his imaginary credit is exhausted and that he will not jump, and in the end nobody gives a damn whether he jumps or not because the real event is already left behind.

This is the problem with anticipation. Is there still a chance that something which has been meticulously programmed will occur? Does a truth which has been meticulously demonstrated still have a chance of being true? When too many things point in the same direction, when the objective reasons pile up, the effect is reversed. Thus everything which points to war is ambiguous: the build-up of force, the play of tension, the concentration of weapons, even the green light from the UN. Far from reinforcing the probability of the conflict, these function as a preventative accumulation, as a substitution for and diversion from the transition to war.

Virtual for five months, the war will shortly enter its terminal phase, according to the rule which says that what never began ends without having taken place. The profound indeterminacy of this war stems from the fact of its being both terminated in advance and interminable. The virtual succeeds itself — accidents aside, which could only be the irruption of the other in the field. But no-one wants to hear talk of the other. Ultimately, the undecidability of the war is grounded in the disappearance of alterity, of primitive hostility, and of the enemy. War has become a celibate machine.

Thanks to this war, the extraordinary confusion in the Arab world is in the process of infecting the West — just revenge. In return, we try desperately to unify and stabilise them in order to exercise better control. It is an historic arm-wrestle: who will stabilise the other before being destabilised themselves? Confronted by the virulent and ungraspable instability of the Arabs and of Islam, whose defence is that of the hysteric in all his versatility, the West is in the process of demonstrating that its values can no longer lay claim to any universality than that (extremely fragile) of the UN.

Faced with the Western logic of under-compensation (the West tends towards the euphemisation and even the inhibition of its power), the Oriental logic of Saddam responds with overcompensation. Although far from having proved himself against Iran, he attacks the West. He operates beyond the reach of his own forces, there where only God can help him. He undertakes an act of magical provocation and it is left to God, or some other predestined connection, to do the rest (this was in principle the role allotted to the Arab masses).

By contrast, through a kind of egocentric generosity or stupidity, the Americans can only imagine and combat an enemy in their own image. They are at once both missionaries and converts of their own way of life, which they triumphally project onto the world. They cannot imagine the Other, nor therefore personally make war upon it. What they make war upon is the alterity of the other, and what they want is to reduce that alterity, to convert it or failing that to annihilate it if it proves irreducible (the Indians). They cannot imagine that conversion and repentance, borne by their own good will, should have no echo in the other, and they are literally disturbed when they see Saddam playing with them and refusing to accede to their reasons. This is perhaps why they have decided to annihilate him, not out of hatred or calculation, but for the crime of felony, treachery, malevolent will and trickery (exactly as with the Indians).

For their part, the Israelis have no such tenderness. They see the Other in all its bare adversity without illusions or scruples. The Other, the Arab, is unconvertible, his alterity is without appeal; it must not be changed, it must be beaten down and subjugated. In doing so, however, while they may not understand they at least recognise it. The Americans, for their part, understand nothing and do not even recognise this fact.

It is not an important match which is being played out in the Gulf, between Western hegemony and the challenge from the rest of the world. It is the West in conflict with itself, by means of an interposed mercenary, after having been in conflict with Islam (Iran), also by means of an interposed Saddam. Saddam remains the fake enemy. At first the champion of the West against Islam, then the champion of Islam against the West. In both cases he is a traitor to his own cause since, even more than the few thousand incidental Westerners, it is the Arab masses that he holds hostage, captures for his own profit and immobilises in their suicidal enthusiasm. It is moreover towards Christmas, at the very moment when he frees the hostages (thereby skilfully stroking the Westerners with the same demagogy that he strokes the children in front of the TV), that he launches his call to the Arab people on the holy war.

It is thus a mistake to think that he would contribute to the unification of the Arab world and to honour him for that. In fact, he only did it to hoodwink them, to make them work for him, to deceive them once again and to render them powerless. People like him are necessary from time to time in order to channel irruptive forces. They serve as a poultice or an artifical purgative. It is a form of deterrence, certainly a Western strategy, but one of which Saddam, in his pride and his stupidity, is a perfect executant. He who loves decoys so much is himself no more than a decoy and his elimination can only demystify this war by putting an end to that objective complicity which itself is no decoy.

But, for this very reason, is the West determined to eliminate him?

The exhibition of American prisoners on Iraqi TV. Once more the politics of blackmail, of hostages, the humiliation of the USA by the spectacle of those "repentants" forced to avow symbolically American dishonour. Our own as well, we whom the screens submit to the same violence, that of the battered, manipulated and powerless prisoner, that of forced voyeurism in response to the forced exhibitionism of the images. Along with the spectacle of these prisoners or these hostages, the screens offer us the spectacle of our powerlessness. In a case such as this, information exactly fulfills its role which is to convince us of our own abjection by the obscenity of what is seen. The forced perversion of the look amounts to the avowal of our own dishonour, and makes repentants of us as well.

That the Americans should have allowed themselves to be ridiculed without departing from their own program and war indicates a weakness in their symbolic detonator. Humiliation remains the worst kind of test, arrogance (Saddam's) the worst kind of conduct, blackmail the worst kind of relationship and the acceptance of blackmail the worst kind of dishonour. The fact that this symbolic violence, worse than any sexual violence, should finally have been withstood without flinching testifies to the depth or the unconscious character of Western masochism. This is the rule of the American way of life: *nothing personal!* And they make war in the same manner: pragmatically and not symbolically. They thereby expose themselves to deadly situations which they are unable to confront. But perhaps they accept this in expiation of their power, in an equivalence which is after all symbolic?

Two intense images, two or perhaps three scenes which all concern disfigured forms or costumes which correspond to the
masquerade of this war: the CNN journalists with their gas
masks in the Jerusalem studios; the drugged and beaten prisoners repenting on the screen of Iraqi TV; and perhaps that sea-
bird covered in oil and pointing its blind eyes towards the Gulf
sky. It is a masquerade of information: branded faces delivered
over to the prostitution of the image, the image of an unintelligible distress. No images of the field of battle, but images of
masks, of blind or defeated faces, images of falsification. It is not
war taking place over there but the disfiguration of the world.

There is a profound scorn in the kind of "clean" war which renders the other powerless without destroying its flesh, which
makes it a point of honour to disarm and neutralise but not to
kill. In a sense, it is worse than the other kind of war because it
spares life. It is like humiliation: by taking less than life it is
worse than taking life. There is undoubtedly a political error
here, in so far as it is acceptable to be defeated but not to be put
out of action. In this manner, the Americans inflict a particular
insult by not making war on the other but simply eliminating
him, the same as one would by not bargaining over the price of
an object and thereby refusing any personal relationship with
the vendor. The one whose price you accept without discussion
despises you. The one whom you disarm without seeing is
insulted and must be avenged. There is perhaps something of
this in the presentation of those humiliated captives on television. It is in a sense to say to America: you who do not wish to

see us, we will show you what you are like.

Just as the psychical or the screen of the psyche transforms
every illness into a symptom (there is no organic illness which
does not find its meaning elsewhere, in an interpretation of the
ailment on another level: all the symptoms pass through a sort
of black box in which the psychic images are jumbled and
inverted, the illness becomes reversible, ungraspable, escaping
any form of realistic medicine), so war, when it has been turned
into information, ceases to be a realistic war and becomes a virtual war, in some way symptomatic. And just as everything
psychical becomes the object of interminable speculation, so
everything which is turned into information becomes the
object of endless speculation, the site of total uncertainty. We
are left with the symptomatic reading on our screens of the
effects of the war, or the effects of discourse about the war, or
completely speculative strategic evaluations which are analo-
gous to those evaluations of opinion provided by polls. In this
manner, we have gone in a week from 20% to 50% and then to
30% destruction of Iraqi military potential. The figure fluctu-
ates exactly like the fortunes of the stock market. "The land
offensive is anticipated today, tomorrow, in a few hours, in any
case sometime this week ... the climatic conditions are ideal for
a confrontation, etc." Whom to believe? There is nothing to
believe. We must learn to read symptoms as symptoms, and
television as the hysterical symptom of a war which has nothing to do with its critical mass. Moreover, it does not seem to
have to reach its critical mass but remains in its inertial phase,

while the implosion of the apparatus of information along with the accompanying tendency of the rate of information to fall seems to reinforce the implosion of war itself, with its accompanying tendency of the rate of confrontation to fall.

Information is like an unintelligent missile which never finds its target (nor, unfortunately, its anti-missile!), and therefore crashes anywhere or gets lost in space on an unpredictable orbit in which it eternally revolves as junk.

Information is only ever an erratic missile with a fuzzy destination which seeks its target but is drawn to every decoy — it is itself a decoy, in fact it scatters all over the environs and the result is mostly nil. The utopia of a targetted promotion or targetted information is the same as that of the targetted missile: it knows not where it lands and perhaps its mission is not to land but, like the missile, essentially to have been launched (as its name indicates). In fact, the only impressive images of missiles, rockets or satellites are those of the launch. It is the same with promotions or five year plans: the campaign launch is what counts, the impact or the end results are so uncertain that one frequently hears no more about them. The entire effect is in the programming, the success is that of the virtual model. Consider the Scuds: their strategic effectiveness is nil and their only (psychological) effect lies in the fact that Saddam succeeded in launching them.

The fact that the production of decoys has become an important branch of the war industry, just as the production of placebos has become an important branch of the medical

industry and forgery a flourishing branch of the art industry —
not to mention the fact that information has become a privi-
leged branch of industry as such — all of this is a sign that we
have entered a deceptive world in which an entire culture
labours assiduously at its counterfeit. This also means that it no
longer harbours any illusion about itself.

It all began with the leitmotif of precision, of surgical, mathe-
matical and punctual efficacy, which is another way of not
recognising the enemy as such, just as lobotomy is a way of not
recognising madness as such. And then all that technical virtu-
osity finished up in the most ridiculous uncertainty. The isola-
tion of the enemy by all kinds of electronic interference creates
a sort of barricade behind which he becomes invisible. He also
becomes "stealthy," and his capacity for resistance becomes
indeterminable. In annihilating him at a distance and as it
were by transparency, it becomes impossible to discern
whether or not he is dead.

The idea of a clean war, like that of a clean bomb or an intelli-
gent missile, this whole war conceived as a technological
extrapolation of the brain is a sure sign of madness. It is like
those characters in Hieronymus Bosch with a glass bell or a
soap bubble around their head as a sign of their mental debility.
A war enclosed in a glass coffin, like Snow White, purged of
any carnal contamination or warrior's passion. A clean war
which ends up in an oil slick.

The French supplied the planes and the nuclear power stations, the Russians the tanks, the English the underground bunkers and runways, the Germans the gas, the Dutch the gas masks, while the Italians supplied the decoy equivalents of everything — tanks, bunkers, inflatable bombers, missiles with artificial thermal emissions, etc. Before so many marvels, one is drawn to compete in diabolical imagination: why not false gas masks for the Palestinians? Why not put the hostages at decoy strategic sites, a fake chemical factory for example?

Has a French plane been downed? The question becomes burning, it is our honour which is at stake. That would constitute a proof of our involvement, and the Iraqis appear to take a malicious pleasure in denying it (perhaps they have a more accurate idea of our involvement?). Whatever the situation, it will be necessary here too to set up decoys, simulated losses and *trompe l'oeil* victims (as with the fake destruction of civic buildings in Timisoara or Baghdad).

A war of high technological concentration but poor definition. Perhaps it has gone beyond its critical mass by too strong a concentration?

Fine illustration of the communication schema in which emitter and receiver on opposite sides of the screen, never connect with each other. Instead of messages, it is missiles and bombs which fly from one side to the other, but any dual or personal relation is altogether absent. Thus an aerial attack on

Iraq may be read in terms of coding, decoding and feedback (in this case, very bad: we cannot even know what we have destroyed). This explains the tolerance of the Israelis: they have only been hit by abstract projectiles, namely missiles. The least live bombing attack on Israel would have provoked immediate retaliation.

Communication is also a clean relation: in principle, it excludes any violent or personal affect. It is strange to see this disaffection, this profound indifference to one another, played out at the very heart of violence and war.

The fact that the undetectable Stealth bombers should have begun the war by aiming at decoys and undoubtedly destroying fake objectives, that the Secret Services (also "furtive") should have been so mistaken in so many ways about the realities of Iraqi weaponry, and the strategists so wrong about the effects of the intensive electronic war, all testifies to the illusionism of force once it is no longer measured against an adversary but against its abstract operation alone. All the generals, admirals and other meretricious experts should be sent to an inflatable strategic site, to see whether these decoys wouldn't in fact attract a real bomb on their heads.

Conversely, the Americans' innocence in admitting their mistake (declaring five months later that the Iraqi forces are almost intact while they themselves are not ready to attack) and all that counter-propaganda which adds to the confusion would be moving if it did not testify to the same strategic idiocy as the triumphal declarations at the outset, and did not further take us for complicit witnesses of this suspicious sincerity of the kind which says: you see, we tell you everything. We can always give credit to the Americans for knowing how to exploit their failures by means of a sort of *trompe l'oeil* candour.

A UN bedtime story: the UN awoke (or was awakened) from its glass coffin (the building in New York). As the coffin fell and was shattered (at the same time as the Eastern Bloc), she spat out the apple and revived, as fresh as a rose, only to find at once the waiting Prince Charming: the Gulf War, also fresh from the arms of the cold war after a long period of mourning. No doubt together they will give birth to a New World Order, or else end up like two ghosts locked in vampiric embrace.

Seeing how Saddam uses his cameras on the hostages, the caressed children, the (fake) strategic targets, on his own smiling face, on the ruins of the milk factory, one cannot help thinking that in the West we still have a hypocritical vision of television and information, to the extent that, despite all the evidence, we hope for their proper use. Saddam, for his part, knows what the media and information are: he makes a radical, unconditional, perfectly cynical and therefore perfectly instrumental use of them. The Romanians too were able to make a perfectly immoral and mystificatory use of them (from our point of view). We may regret this, but given the principle of simulation which governs all information, even the most pious and objective, and given the structural unreality of images and their proud indifference to the truth, these cynics alone are right about information when they employ it as an unconditional simulacrum. We believe that they immorally pervert images. Not so. They alone are conscious of the profound immorality of images, just as the Bokassas and Amin Dadas reveal, through the parodic and Ubuesque use they make of them, the obscene truth of the Western political and democratic structures they borrowed. The secret of the underdeveloped is to parody their model and render it ridiculous by exaggeration. We alone retain the illusion of information and of a right to information. They are not so naive.

Never any acting out, or passage to action, but simply acting: roll cameras! But there is too much film, or none at all, or it was desensitised by remaining too long in the humidity of the cold war. In short, there is quite simply nothing to see. Later, there will be something to see for the viewers of archival cassettes and the generations of video-zombies who will never cease reconstituting the event, never having had the intuition of the non-event of this war.

The archive also belongs to virtual time; it is the complement of the event "in real time," of that instantaneity of the event and its diffusion. Moreover, rather than the "revolution" of real time of which Virilio speaks, we should speak of an involution in real time; of an involution of the event in the instantaneity of everything at once, and of its vanishing in information itself. If we take note of the speed of light and the temporal short-circuit of pure war (the nanosecond), we see that this involution precipitates us precisely into the virtuality of war and not into its reality, it precipitates us into the absence of war. Must we denounce the speed of light?

Utopia of real time which renders the event simultaneous at all points on the globe. In fact, what we live in real time is not the event, but rather in larger than life (in other words, in the virtual size of the image) the spectacle of the degradation of the event and its spectral evocation (the "spiritualism of information": event, are you there? Gulf War, are you there?) in the commentary, gloss, and verbose *mise en scène* of talking heads which only underlines the impossibility of the image and the correlative unreality of the war. It is the same aporia as that of *cinéma vérité* which seeks to short-circuit the unreality of the image in order to present us the truth of the object. In this manner, CNN seeks to be a stethoscope attached to the hypothetical heart of the war, and to present us with its hypothetical pulse. But this auscultation only provides a confused ultrasound, undecidable symptoms, and an assortment of vague and contradictory diagnoses. All that we can hope for is to see them die live (metaphorically of course), in other words that some event or other should overwhelm the information instead of the information inventing the event and commenting artificially upon it. The only real information revolution would be this one, but it is not likely to occur in the near future: it would presuppose a reversal of the idea we have of information. In the meantime, we will continue with the involution and encrustation of the event in and by information, and the closer we approach the live and real time, the further we will go in this direction.

The same illusion of progress occurred with the appearance of speech and then colour on screen: at each stage of this progress we moved further away from the imaginary intensity of the image. The closer we supposedly approach the real or the truth, the further we draw away from them both, since neither one nor the other exists. The closer we approach the real time of the event, the more we fall into the illusion of the virtual. God save us from the illusion of war.

At a certain speed, the speed of light, you lose even your shadow. At a certain speed, the speed of information, things lose their sense. There is a great risk of announcing (or denouncing) the Apocalypse of real time, when it is precisely at this point that the event volatilises and becomes a black hole from which light no longer escapes. War implodes in real time, history implodes in real time, all communication and all signification implode in real time. The Apocalypse itself, understood as the arrival of catastrophe, is unlikely. It falls prey to the prophetic illusion. The world is not sufficiently coherent to lead to the Apocalypse.

Nevertheless, in confronting our opinions on the war with the diametrically opposed opinions of Paul Virilio, one of us betting on apocalyptic escalation and the other on deterrence and the indefinite virtuality of war, we concluded that this decidedly strange war went in both directions at once. The war's programmed escalation is relentless and its non-occurrence no less inevitable: the war proceeds at once towards the two extremes of intensification and deterrence. The war and the non-war

take place at the same time, with the same period of deployment and suspense and the same possibilities of de-escalation
or maximal increase.

What is most extraordinary is that the two hypotheses, the
apocalypse of real time and pure war along with the triumph of
the virtual over the real, are realised at the same time, in the
same space-time, each in implacable pursuit of the other. It is a
sign that the space of the event has become a hyperspace with
multiple refractivity, and that *the space of war has become definitively non-Euclidean.* And that there will undoubtedly be no resolution of this situation: we will remain in the undecidability of
war, which is the undecidability created by the unleashing of
the two opposed principles.

Soft war and pure war go boating.

There is a degree of popular good will in the micro-panic dis-
tilled by the airwaves. The public ultimately consents to be
frightened, and to be gently terrorised by the bacteriological
scenarios, on the basis of a kind of affective patriotism, even
while it preserves a fairly profound indifference to the war. But
it censors this indifference, on the grounds that we must not
cut ourselves off from the world scene, that we must be
mobilised at least as extras in order to rescue war: we have no
other passion with which to replace it. It is the same with political participation under normal circumstances: this is largely
second hand, taking place against a backdrop of spontaneous
indifference. It is the same with God: even when we no longer
believe, we continue to believe that we believe. In this hysteri-

cal replacement function, we identify at once those who are superfluous and they are many. By contrast, the few who advance the hypothesis of this profound indifference will be received as traitors.

By the force of the media, this war liberates an exponential mass of stupidity, not the particular stupidity of war, which is considerable, but the professional and functional stupidity of those who pontificate in perpetual commentary on the event: all the Bouvards and Pécuchets for hire, the would-be raiders of the lost image, the CNN types and all the master singers of strategy and information who make us experience the emptiness of television as never before. This war, it must be said, constitutes a merciless test. Fortunately, no one will hold this expert or general or that intellectual for hire to account for the idiocies or absurdities proffered the day before, since these will be erased by those of the following day. In this manner, everyone is amnestied by the ultra-rapid succession of phony events and phony discourses. The laundering of stupidity by the escalation of stupidity which reconstitutes a sort of total innocence, namely the innocence of washed and bleached brains, stupefied not by the violence but by the sinister insignificance of the images.

French defense minister who resigned in opposition to Gulf Coalition

Chevènement in the desert: *Morituri te salutant!* Ridiculous. France with its old Jaguars and its presidential slippers.

Capillon on television: the benefit of this war will have been to recycle our military leaders on television. One shudders at the thought that in another time, in a real war, they were operational on the battlefield.

Imbroglio: that pacifist demonstration in Paris, thus indirectly for Saddam Hussein, who does want war, and against the French Government which does not want it, and which from the outset gives all the signs of refusing to take part, or of doing so reluctantly.

Deserted shops, suspended vacations, the slowdown of activity, the city turned over to the absent masses: it may well be that, behind the alibi of panic, this war should be the dreamed-for opportunity to soft-pedal, the opportunity to slow down, to ease off the pace. The crazed particles calm down, the war erases the guerrilla warfare of everyday life. Catharsis? No: renovation. Or perhaps, with everyone glued at home, TV plays out fully its role of social control by collective stupefaction: turning uselessly upon itself like a dervish, it affixes populations all the better for deceiving them, as with a bad detective novel which we cannot believe could be so pointless.

Iraq is being rebuilt even before it has been destroyed. After-sales service. Such anticipation reduces even further the credibility of the war, which did not need this to discourage those who wanted to believe in it.

Sometimes a glimmer of black humour: the twelve thousand coffins sent along with the arms and ammunition. Here too, the Americans demonstrate their presumption: their projections and their losses are without common measure. But Saddam challenged them with being incapable of sacrificing ten thousand men in a war: they replied by sending twelve thousand coffins.

The overestimation of losses is part of the same megalomaniac light show as the publicised deployment of "Desert Shield" and the orgy of bombardment. The pilots no longer even have any targets. The Iraqis no longer even have enough decoys to cater for the incessant raids. The same target must be bombed five times. Mockery.

The British artillery unleashed for twenty four hours. Long since there was nothing left to destroy. Why then? In order "to cover the noise of the armoured columns advancing towards the front by the noise of the bombardment." Of course, the effect of surprise must be maintained (it is February 21). The best part is that there was no longer anyone there, the Iraqis had already left. Absurdity.

Saddam is a mercenary, the Americans are missionaries. But once the mercenary is beaten, the missionaries become *de facto* the mercenaries of the entire world. But the price for becoming a perfect mercenary is to be stripped of all political intelligence and all will. The Americans cannot escape it: if they want to be the police of the world and the New World Order, they must lose all political authority in favour of their operational capacity alone. They will become pure executants and everyone else pure extras in the consensual and policed New World Order.

Whoever the dictator to be destroyed, any punitive force sure of itself is even more frightening. Having assumed the Israeli style, the Americans will henceforth export it everywhere and, just as the Israelis did, lock themselves into the spiral of unconditional repression.

For the Americans, the enemy does not exist as such. *Nothing personal.* Your war is of no interest to me, your resistance is of no interest to me. I will destroy you when I am ready. Refusal to bargain, whereas Saddam Hussein, for his part, bargains his war by overbidding in order to fall back, attempting to force the hand by pressure and blackmail, like a hustler trying to sell his goods. The Americans understand nothing in this whole psychodrama of bargaining, they are had every time until, with the wounded pride of the Westerner, they stiffen and impose their conditions. They understand nothing of this floating duel, this passage of arms in which, for a brief moment, the honour and dishonour of each is in play. They know only their virtue, and they are proud of their virtue. If the other wants to play, to trick and to challenge, they will virtuously employ their force. They will oppose the other's traps with their character armour and their armoured tanks. For them, the time of exchange does not exist. But the other, even if he knows that he will concede, cannot do so without another form of procedure. He must be recognised as interlocutor: this is the goal of the exchange. He must be recognised as an enemy: this is the whole aim of the war. For the Americans, bargaining is cheap whereas for the others it is a matter of honour, (mutual) personal recognition, linguistic strategy (language exists, it must be honoured) and respect for time (altercation demands a rhythm, it is the price of there being an Other). The Americans take no account of these primitive subtleties. They have much to learn about symbolic exchange.

By contrast, they are winners from an economic point of view. No time lost in discussion, no psychological risk in any duel with the other: it is a way of proving that time does not exist, that the other does not exist, and that all that matters is the model and mastery of the model.

From a military point of view, to allow this war to endure in the way they have (instead of applying an Israeli solution and immediately exploiting the imbalance of force while short-circuiting all retaliatory effects), is a clumsy solution lacking in glory and full of perverse effects (Saddam's aura among the Arab masses). Nevertheless, in doing this, they impose a suspense, a temporal vacuum in which they present to themselves and to the entire world the spectacle of their virtual power. They will have allowed the war to endure as long as it takes, not to win but to persuade the whole world of the infallibility of their machine.

The victory of the model is more important than victory on the ground. Military success consecrates the triumph of arms, but the programming success consecrates the defeat of time. War-processing, the transparency of the model in the unfolding of the war, the strategy of relentless execution of a program, the electrocution of all reaction and any live initiative, including their own: these are more important from the point of view of general deterrence (of friends and foes alike) than the final result on the ground. Clean war, white war, programmed war: more lethal than the war which sacrifices human lives.

We are a long way from annihilation, holocaust and atomic apocalypse, the total war which functions as the archaic imaginary of media hysteria. On the contrary, this kind of preventative, deterrent and punitive war is a warning to everyone not to take extreme measures and inflict upon themselves what they inflict on others (the missionary complex): the rule of the game that says everyone must remain within the limits of their power and not make war by any means whatever. Power must remain virtual and exemplary, in other words, virtuous. The decisive test is the planetary apprenticeship in this regulation. Just as wealth is no longer measured by the ostentation of wealth but by the secret circulation of speculative capital, so war is not measured by being waged but by its speculative unfolding in an abstract, electronic and informational space, the same space in which capital moves.

While this conjuncture does not exclude all accident (disorder in the virtual), it is nevertheless true that the probability of the irruption of those extreme measures and mutual violence which we call war is increasingly low.

Saddam the hysteric. Interminable shit kicker. The hysteric cannot be crushed: he is reborn from his symptoms as though from his ashes. Confronted by a hysteric, the other becomes paranoid, he deploys a massive apparatus of protection and

mistrust. He suspects the hysteric of bad faith, of ruse and dissimulation. He wants to constrain him to the truth and to
transparency. The hysteric is irreducible. His means are decoys
and the overturning of alliances. Confronted with this lubricity,
this duplicity, the paranoid can only become more rigid, more
obsessional. The most violent reproach addressed to Saddam
Hussein by Bush is that of being a liar, a traitor, a bad player, a
trickster. *Lying son of a bitch!* Saddam, like a good hysteric, has
never given birth to his own war: for him, it is only a phantom
pregnancy. By contrast, he has until now succeeded in prevent-
ing Bush from giving birth to his. And, with the complicity of
Gorbachev, he almost succeeded in fucking him up the ass. But
the hysteric is not suicidal, this is the advantageous other side
to Saddam. He is neither mad nor suicidal. perhaps he should
be treated by hypnosis?

The Iraqis and the Americans have at least one thing in common, a heinous crime which they (and with them the West)
share. Many things about this war are explained by this anteri-
or crime from which both sides sought to profit with impunity.
The secret expiation of this crime feeds the Gulf War in its confusion and its allure of the settling of accounts. Such is the
shared agreement to forget it that little is spoken about this
prior episode (even by the Iranians), namely the war against
Iran. Saddam must avenge his failure to win, even though he
was the aggressor and sure of his impunity. He must avenge
himself against the West which trained him for it, while the
Americans, for their part, must suppress him as the embarrass-

ing accomplice in that criminal act.

For any government official or despot, power over his own people takes precedence over everything else. In the case of the Gulf War, this provides the only chance of a solution or a de-escalation. Saddam will prefer to concede rather than destroy his internal hegemony or sacrifice his army, etc. In this sense, sheltering his planes in Iran is a good sign: rather than an offensive sign, it is the ploy of a burglar who stashes his haul in order to retrieve it when he comes out of prison, thus an argument against any heroic or suicidal intention.

While one fraction of the intellectuals and politicians, specialists in the reserve army of mental labour, are whole-heartedly in favour of the war, and another fraction are against it from the bottom of their hearts, but for reasons no less disturbing, all are agreed on one point: this war exists, we have seen it. There is no interrogation into the event itself or its reality; or into the fraudulence of this war, the programmed and always delayed illusion of battle; or into the machination of this war and its amplification by information, not to mention the improbable orgy of material, the systematic manipulation of data, the artificial dramatisation ... If we do not have practical intelligence about the war (and none among us has), at least let us have a sceptical intelligence towards it, without renouncing the pathetic feeling of its absurdity.

But there is more than one kind of absurdity: that of the massacre and that of being caught up in the illusion of massacre. It is just as in La Fontaine's fable: the day there is a real war you will not even be able to tell the difference. The real victory of the simulators of war is to have drawn everyone into this rotten simulation.

B. complains of a virtual war as if he's playing chicken. Does he want a "real" war?

The Gulf War
did not take place

Since this war was won in advance, we will never know what it would have been like had it existed. We will never know what an Iraqi taking part with a chance of fighting would have been like. We will never know what an American taking part with a chance of being beaten would have been like. We have seen what an ultra-modern process of electrocution is like, a process of paralysis or lobotomy of an experimental enemy away from the field of battle with no possibility of reaction. But this is not a war, any more than 10,000 tonnes of bombs per day is sufficient to make it a war. Any more than the direct transmission by CNN of real time information is sufficient to authenticate a war. One is reminded of *Capricorn One* in which the flight of a manned rocket to Mars, which only took place in a desert studio, was relayed live to all the television stations in the world.

It has been called a surgical war, and it is true that there is something in common between this *in vitro* destruction and *in vitro* fertilisation — the latter also produces a living being but it is not sufficient to produce a child. Except in the New Genetic Order, a child issues from sexual copulation. Except in the New World Order, war is born of an antagonistic, destructive but dual relation between two adversaries. This war is an asexual surgical war, a matter of war-processing in which the enemy only appears as a computerised target, just as sexual partners only appear as code-names on the screen of *Minitel Rose*. If we can speak of sex in the latter case then perhaps the Gulf War can pass for a war.

The Iraqis blow up civilian buildings in order to give the impression of a dirty war. The Americans disguise satellite information to give the impression of a clean war. Everything in *trompe l'oeil*! The final Iraqi ploy: to secretly evacuate Kuwait and thereby mock the great offensive. With hindsight, the Presidential Guard itself was perhaps only a mirage; in any case, it was exploited as such until the end. All this is no more than a stratagem and the war ended in general boredom, or worse in the feeling of having been duped. Iraqi boasting, American hypocrisy. It is as though there was a virus infecting this war from the beginning which emptied it of all credibility. It is perhaps because the two adversaries did not even confront each other face to face, the one lost in its virtual war won in advance, the other buried in its traditional war lost in advance. They never saw each other: when the Americans finally appeared behind their curtain of bombs the Iraqis had already disappeared behind their curtain of smoke ...

The general effect is of a farce which we will not even have had time to applaud. The only escalation will have been in decoys, opening onto the final era of great confrontations which vanish in the mist. The events in Eastern Europe still gave the impression of a divine surprise. No such thing in the Gulf, where it is as though events were devoured in advance by the parasite virus, the retro-virus of history. This is why we could advance the hypothesis that this war would not take place. And now that it is over, we can realise at last that it did not take place.

It was buried for too long, whether in the concrete and sand Iraqi bunkers or in the Americans' electronic sky, or behind that other form of sepulchre, the chattering television screens. Today everything tends to go underground, including information in its informational bunkers. Even war has gone underground in order to survive. In this forum of war which is the Gulf, everything is hidden: the planes are hidden, the tanks are buried, Israel plays dead, the images are censored and all information is blockaded in the desert: only TV functions as a medium without a message, giving at last the image of pure television.

Like an animal, the war goes to ground. It hides in the sand, it hides in the sky. It is like the Iraqi planes: it knows that it has no chance if it surfaces. It awaits its hour ... which will never come.

The Americans themselves are the vectors of this catalepsy. There is no question that the war came from their plan and its programmed unfolding. No question that, in their war, the Iraqis went to war. No question that the Other came from their computers. All reaction, even on their part (as we saw in the episode of the prisoners, which should have produced a violent reaction), all abreaction against the program, all improvisation is abolished (even the Israelis were muzzled). What is tested here in this foreclosure of the enemy, this experimental reclusion of war, is the future validity for the entire planet of this type of suffocating and machinic performance, virtual and relentless in its unfolding. In this perspective, war could not take place. There is no more room for war than for any form of living impulse.

War stripped of its passions, its phantasms, its finery, its veils, its violence, its images; war stripped bare by its technicians even, and then reclothed by them with all the artifices of electronics, as though with a second skin. But these too are a kind of decoy that technology sets up before itself. Saddam Hussein's decoys still aim to deceive the enemy, whereas the American technological decoy only aims to deceive itself. The first days of the lightning attack, dominated by this technological mystification, will remain one of the finest bluffs, one of the finest collective mirages of contemporary History (along with Timisoara). We are all accomplices in these fantasmagoria, it must be said, as we are in any publicity campaign. In the past, the unemployed constituted the reserve army of Capital; today, in our enslavement to information, we constitute the reserve army of all planetary mystifications.

Saddam constructed his entire war as a decoy (whether deliberately or not), including the decoy of defeat which even more resembles a hysterical syncope of the type: peek-a-boo, I am no longer there! But the Americans also constructed their affair as a decoy, like a parabolic mirror of their own power, taking no account of what was before them, or hallucinating those opposite to be a threat of comparable size to themselves: otherwise they would not even have been able to believe in their own victory. Their victory itself in the form of a triumphal decoy echoes the Iraqi decoy of defeat. Ultimately, both were accomplices as thick as thieves, and we were collectively abused. This is why the war remains indefinable and ungraspable, all strategy having given way to stratagem.

One of the two adversaries is a rug salesman, the other an arms salesman: they have neither the same logic nor the same strategy, even though they are both crooks. There is not enough communication between them to enable them to make war upon each other. Saddam will never fight, while the Americans will fight against a fictive double on screen. They see Saddam as he should be, a modernist hero, worth defeating (the fourth biggest army in the world!). Saddam remains a rug salesman who takes the Americans for rug salesmen like himself, stronger than he but less gifted for the scam. He hears nothing of deterrence. For there to be deterrence, there must be communication. It is a game of rational strategy which presupposes real time communication between the two adversaries; whereas in this war there was never communication at any moment, but always dislocation in time, Saddam evolving in a long time, that of blackmail, of procrastination, false advance, of retreat: the recurrent time of *The Thousand and One Nights* — exactly the inverse of real time. Deterrence in fact presupposes a virtual escalation between the two adversaries. By contrast, Saddam's entire strategy rests upon de-escalation (one sets a maximal price then descends from it in stages). And their respective denouements are not at all the same. The failure of the sales pitch is marked by evasive action: the salesman rolls up his rug and leaves. Thus, Saddam disappears without further ado. The failure of deterrence is marked by force: this is the case with the Americans. Once again, there is no relation between the two, each plays in his own space and misses the other. We cannot even say that the Americans defeated Saddam: he defaulted on them, he de-escalated and they were not able to escalate sufficiently to destroy him.

Finally, who could have rendered more service to everyone, in such a short time at such little cost, than Saddam Hussein? He reinforced the security of Israel (reflux of the Intifada, revival of world opinion for Israel), assured the glory of American arms, gave Gorbachev a political chance, opened the door to Iran and Shiism, relaunched the UN, etc., all for free since he alone paid the price of blood. Can we conceive of so admirable a man? And he did not even fall! He remains a hero for the Arab masses. It is as though he were an agent of the CIA disguised as Saladin.

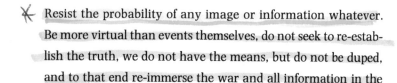 Resist the probability of any image or information whatever. Be more virtual than events themselves, do not seek to re-establish the truth, we do not have the means, but do not be duped, and to that end re-immerse the war and all information in the

virtuality from whence they come. Turn deterrence back against itself. Be meteorologically sensitive to stupidity.

In the case of this war, it is a question of the living illustration of an implacable logic which renders us incapable of envisaging any hypothesis other than that of its real occurrence. The realist logic which lives on the illusion of the final result. The denial of the facts is never one of them. The final resolution of an equation as complex as a war is never immediately apparent in the war. It is a question of seizing the logic of its unfolding, in the absence of any prophetic illusion. To be for or against the war is idiotic if the question of the very probability of this war, its credibility or degree of reality has not been raised even for a moment. All political and ideological speculations fall under mental deterrence (stupidity). By virtue of their immediate consensus on the evidence they feed the unreality of this war, they reinforce its bluff by their unconscious dupery.

The real warmongers are those who live on the ideology of the veracity of this war, while the war itself wreaks its havoc at another level by trickery, hyperreality, simulacra, and by the entire mental strategy of deterrence which is played out in the facts and in the images, in the anticipation of the real by the virtual, of the event by virtual time, and in the inexorable confusion of the two. All those who understand nothing of this involuntarily reinforce this halo of bluff which surrounds us.

It is as though the Iraqis were electrocuted, lobotomised, running towards the television journalists in order to surrender or immobilised beside their tanks, not even demoralised: de-cerebralised, stupefied rather than defeated — can this be called a war? Today we see the shreds of this war rot in the desert just like the shreds of the map in Borges' fable rotting at the four corners of the territory (moreover, strangely, he situates his fable in the same oriental regions of the Empire).

Fake war, deceptive war, not even the illusion but the disillusion of war, linked not only to defensive calculation, which translates into the monstrous prophylaxis of this military machine, but also to the mental disillusion of the combatants themselves, and to the global disillusion of everyone else by means of information. For deterrence is a total machine (it is the true war machine), and it not only operates at the heart of the event — where electronic coverage of the war devoured time and space, where virtuality (the decoy, programming, the anticipation of the end) devoured all the oxygen of war like a fuel-air explosive bomb — it also operates in our heads. Information has a profound function of deception. It matters little what it "informs" us about, its "coverage" of events matters little since it is precisely no more than a cover: its purpose is to produce consensus by flat encephalogram. The complement of the unconditional simulacrum in the field is to train everyone in the unconditional reception of broadcast simulacra. Abolish any intelligence of the event. The result is a suffocating atmosphere of deception and stupidity. And if people are vaguely aware of being caught up in this appeasement and this disillusion by images, they swallow the deception and remain fascinated by the evidence of the montage of this war with which we are inoculated everywhere: through the eyes, the senses and in discourse.

There are ironic balance sheets which help to temper the shock or the bluff of this war. A simple calculation shows that, of the 500,000 American soldiers involved during the seven months of operations in the Gulf, three times as many would have died from road accidents alone had they stayed in civilian life. Should we consider multiplying clean wars in order to reduce the murderous death toll of peacetime?

On this basis, we could develop a philosophy of perverse effects, which we tend to regard as always maleficent whereas in fact maleficent causes (war, illness, viruses) often produce beneficial perverse effects. They are no less perverse as a result, but more interesting than the others, in particular because it has been a matter of principle never to study them. Except for Mandeville, of course, in *The Fable of the Bees*, where he shows that every society prospers on the basis of its vices. But the course of events has drawn us further and further away from an intelligence of this order.

An example: deterrence itself. It only functions well between equal forces. Ideally, each party should possess the same weapons before agreeing to renounce their use. It is therefore the dissemination of (atomic) weapons alone which can ensure effective global deterrence and the indefinite suspension of war. The present politics of non-dissemination plays with fire: there will always be enough madmen to launch an archaic challenge below the level of an atomic riposte — witness Saddam. Things being as they are, we should place our hopes in the spread of weapons rather than in their (never respected) limitation. Here too, the beneficial perverse effect of dissemination should be taken into account. We should escalate in the virtual (of destruction) under penalty of de-escalating in the real. This is the paradox of deterrence. It is like information, culture or other material and spiritual goods: only their profusion renders them indifferent and neutralises their negative perverse effects. Multiply vices in order to ensure the collective good.

That said, the consequences of what did not take place may be as substantial as those of an historical event. The hypothesis would be that, in the case of the Gulf War as in the case of the events in Eastern Europe, we are no longer dealing with "historical events" but with places of collapse. Eastern Europe saw the collapse of communism, the construction of which had indeed been an historic event, borne by a vision of the world and a utopia. By contrast, its collapse is borne by nothing and bears nothing, but only opens onto a confused desert left vacant by the retreat of history and immediately invaded by its refuse.

The Gulf War is also a place of collapse, a virtual and meticulous operation which leaves the same impression of a non-event where the military confrontation fell short and where no political power proved itself. The collapse of Iraq and stupefaction of the Arab world are the consequences of a confrontation which did not take place and which undoubtedly never could take place. But this non-war in the form of a victory also consecrates the Western political collapse throughout the Middle East, incapable even of eliminating Saddam and of imagining or imposing anything apart from this new desert and police order called world order.

what exactly
is new world order?

As a consequence of this non-event and living proof of
Western political weakness, Saddam is indeed still there, once
again what he always was, the mercenary of the West, deserv-
ing punishment for not remaining in his place, but also worthy
of continuing to gas the Kurds and the Shiites since he had the
tact not to employ these weapons against those Western dogs,
and worthy of keeping his Presidential Guard since he had the
heart to not sacrifice them in combat. Miraculously (they were
thought to have been destroyed), the Presidential Guard recov-
ers all its valour against the insurgents. Moreover, it is typical
of Saddam to prove his combativity and ferocity only against
his internal enemies: as with every true dictator, the ultimate
end of politics, carefully masked elsewhere by the effects of
democracy, is to maintain control of one's own people by any
means, including terror. This function embodied by dictator-
ships — that of being politically revealing and at the same time
an alibi for democracies — no doubt explains the inexplicable
weakness of the large powers towards them. Saddam liquidates
the communists, Moscow flirts even more with him; he gasses
the Kurds, it is not held against him; he eliminates the religious
cadres, the whole of Islam makes peace with him. Whence this
impunity? Why are we content to inflict a perfect semblance of
military defeat upon him in exchange for a perfect semblance of
victory for the Americans? This ignominious remounting of
Saddam, replacing him in the saddle after his clown act at the
head of the holy war, clearly shows that on all sides the war is
considered not to have taken place. Even the last phase of this
armed mystification will have changed nothing, for the

100,000 Iraqi dead will only have been the final decoy that Saddam will have sacrificed, the blood money paid in forfeit according to a calculated equivalence, in order to conserve his power. What is worse is that these dead still serve as an alibi for those who do not want to have been excited for nothing, nor to have been had for nothing: at least the dead would prove that this war was indeed a war and not a shameful and pointless hoax, a programmed and melodramatic version of what was the drama of war (Marx once spoke of this second, melodramatic version of a primary event). But we can rest assured that the next soap opera in this genre will enjoy an even fresher and more joyful credulity.

What a job Saddam has done for the Americans, from his combat with Iran up to this full scale debacle! Nevertheless, everything is ambiguous since this collapse removes any demonstrative value from American power, along with any belief in the Western ideologies of modernity, democracy, or secularity, of which Saddam had been made the incarnation in the Arab world.

We can see that the Western powers dreamt of an Islamic perestroika, on the newly formed model of Eastern Europe: democracy irresistibly establishing itself in those countries conquered by the forces of Good. The Arab countries will be liberated (the peoples cannot but want to be liberated), and the women of Saudi Arabia will have the right to drive. Alas! this is not to be.

The conquered have not been convinced and have withdrawn, leaving the victors only the bitter taste of an unreal made-to-order victory. Defeat can also be a rival bid and a new beginning, the chain of implication never stops. The eventual outcome is unpredictable and certainly will not be reckoned in terms of freedom.

No accidents occurred in this war, everything unfolded according to programmatic order, in the absence of passional disorder. Nothing occurred which would have metamorphosed events into a duel.

Even the status of the deaths may be questioned, on both sides. The minimal losses of the coalition pose a serious problem, which never arose in any earlier war. The paltry number of deaths may be cause for self-congratulation, but nothing will prevent this figure being paltry. Strangely, a war without victims does not seem like a real war but rather the prefiguration of an experimental, blank war, or a war even more inhuman because it is without human losses. No heroes on the other side either, where death was most often that of sacrificed extras, left as cover in the trenches of Kuwait, or civilians serving as bait and martyrs for the dirty war. Disappeared, abandoned to their lot, in the thick fog of war, held in utter contempt by their chief, without even the collective glory of a number (we do not know how many they are).

Along with the hostage or the repentant, the figure of the

"disappeared" has become emblematic in our political universe. Before, there were the dead and traitors, now there are the disappeared and the repentant: both blanks. Even the dead are blanks: "We have already buried them, they can no longer be counted," *dixit* Schwarzkopf. At Timisoara, there were too many of them, here there are not enough, but the effect is the same. The non-will to know is part of the non-war. Lies and shame appeared throughout this war like a sexually transmitted disease.

Blank out the war. Just as Kuwait and Iraq were rebuilt before they were destroyed, so at every phase of this war things unfolded as though they were virtually completed. It is not for lack of brandishing the threat of a chemical war, a bloody war, a world war — everyone had their say — as though it were necessary to give ourselves a fright, to maintain everyone in a state of erection for fear of seeing the flaccid member of war fall down. This futile masturbation was the delight of all the TVs. Ordinarily we denounce this kind of behaviour as emphatic or as empty and theatrical affectation: why not denounce an entire event when it is affected by the same hysteria?

In many respects, this war was a scandal of the same type as Timisoara. Not so much the war itself but the manipulation of minds and blackmail by the scenario. The worst scandal being the collective demand for intoxication, the complicity of all in the effects of war, the effects of reality and false transparency in this war. We could almost speak of media harassment along the lines of sexual harassment. Alas! the problem always remains the same and it is insoluble: where does real violence begin, where does consenting violence end? Bluff and information serve as aphrodisiacs for war, just as the corpses at Timisoara and their global diffusion served as aphrodisiacs for the Romanian revolution.

But, ultimately, what have you got against aphrodisiacs? Nothing so long as orgasm is attained. The media mix has become the prerequisite to any orgasmic event. We need it precisely because the event escapes us, because conviction escapes us. We have a pressing need of simulation, even that of war, much more than we have of milk, jam or liberty, and we have an immediate intuition of the means necessary to obtain it. This is indeed the fundamental advance of our democracy: the image-function, the blackmail-function, the information-function, the speculation-function. The obscene aphrodisiac function fulfilled by the decoy of the event, by the decoy of war. Drug-function.

We have neither need of nor the taste for real drama or real war. What we require is the aphrodisiac spice of the multiplication of fakes and the hallucination of violence, for we have a hallucinogenic pleasure in all things, which, as in the case of drugs, is also the pleasure in our indifference and our irresponsibility and thus in our true liberty. Here is the supreme form of democracy. Through it our definitive retreat from the world takes shape: the pleasure of mental speculation in images equalling that of capital in a stock market run, or that of the corpses in the charnel house of Timisoara. But, ultimately, what have you got against drugs?

Nothing. Apart from fact that the collective disillusion is

terrible once the spell is broken; for example, when the corpses at Timisoara were uncovered, or when awareness of the subterfuge of the war takes hold. The scandal today is no longer in the assault on moral values but in the assault on the reality principle. The profound scandal which hereafter infects the whole sphere of information with a Timisoara-complex lay in the compulsory participation of the corpses, the transformation of the corpses into extras which in the same moment transforms all those who saw and believed in it into compulsory extras, so that they themselves become corpses in the charnel house of news signs. The odium lies in the malversation of the real, the faking of the event and the malversation of the war. The charnel houses of Timisoara are such a parody, so paltry by contrast with the real slaughter-houses of history! This Gulf War is such a sham, so paltry: the point is not to rehabilitate other wars, but rather that the recourse to the same pathos is all the more odious when there is no longer even the alibi of a war.

The presumption of information and the media here doubles the political arrogance of the Western empire. All those jour-nalists who set themselves up as bearers of the universal con-science, all those presenters who set themselves up as strate-gists, all the while overwhelming us with a flood of useless images. Emotional blackmail by massacre, fraud. Instead of dis-cussing the threshold of social tolerance for immigration we would do better to discuss the threshold of mental tolerance for information. With regard to the latter, we can say that it was deliberately crossed.

The delirious spectacle of wars which never happened: the transparent glacier of flights which never flew. All these events, from Eastern Europe or from the Gulf, which under the colours of war and liberation led only to political and historical disillusionment (it seems that the famous Chinese Cultural Revolution was the same: a whole strategy of more or less concerted internal destabilisation which short-circuited popular spontaneity), post-synchronisation events where one has the impression of never having seen the original. Bad actors, bad doubles, bad striptease: throughout these seven months, the war has unfolded like a long striptease, following the calculated escalation of undressing and approaching the incandescent point of explosion (like that of erotic effusion) but at the same time withdrawing from it and maintaining a deceptive suspense (teasing), such that when the naked body finally appears, it is no longer naked, desire no longer exists and the orgasm is cut short. In this manner, the escalation was administered to us by drip-feed, removing us further and further from the passage to action and, in any case, from the war. It is like truth according to Nietzsche: we no longer believe that the truth is true when all its veils have been removed. Similarly, we do not believe that war is war when all uncertainty is supposedly removed and it appears as a naked operation. The nudity of war is no less virtual than that of the erotic body in the apparatus of striptease.

On the slopes at Courchevel, the news from the Gulf War is relayed by loudspeakers during the intensive bombardments. Did the others over there, the Iraqis in the sand bunkers receive the snow reports from Courchevel?

February 22 was the day of the Apocalypse: the day of the unleashing of the land offensive behind its curtain of bombs, and in France, by a kind of black humour, the day of the worst traffic jam on the autoroutes to the snow. While the tanks advanced to the assault on Kuwait, the automobile hordes advanced to the assault on the snowfields. Moreover, the tanks went through much more easily than the waves of leisure-seekers. And the dead were more numerous on the snow front than on the war front. Are we so lacking in death, even in time of war, that it must be sought on the playing fields?

Stuck in traffic, one can always amuse oneself by listening to the Gulf radio reports: the time of information never stops, the slower things are on the roads the more things circulate on the wavelengths. Another distraction was that of the young couple who switched between watching the war on TV and their child to be, filmed and recorded in the mother's womb and made available on ultrasound cassette. When the war stops, they watch the kid. At the level of images it is the same combat: war before it has broken out, the child before it has been born. Leisure in the virtual era.

The liquidation of the Shiites and the Kurds by Saddam under the benevolent eye of the American divisions mysteriously stopped in their lightning advance "in order not to humiliate an entire people" offers a bloody analogy with the crushing of the Paris Commune in 1871 under the eye of the Prussian armies. And the good souls who cried out for seven months, for or against the war but always for the good cause, those who denounced the aberrations of the pro-Iraqi policy ten years after the event when it was no longer relevant, and all the repentants of the Rights of Man, once again do nothing. The world accepts this as the wages of defeat, or rather, on the American side, as the wages of victory. The same Americans who, after having dumped hundreds of thousands of tonnes of bombs, today claim to abstain from "intervening in the internal affairs of a State."

It is nevertheless admirable that we call the Arabs and Moslems traditionalists with the same repulsion that we call someone racist, even though we live in a typically traditionalist society although one simultaneously on the way to disintegration. We do not practise hard fundamentalist traditionalism, we practise soft, subtle and shameful democratic traditionalism by consensus. However, consensual traditionalism (that of the Enlightenment, the Rights of Man, the Left in power, the repentant intellectual and sentimental humanism) is every bit as fierce as that of any tribal religion or primitive society.

It denounces the other as absolute Evil in exactly the same manner (these are the words of François Mitterand apropos the Salman Rushdie affair: whence does he derive such an archaic form of thought?). The difference between the two traditionalisms (hard and soft) lies in the fact that our own (the soft) holds all the means to destroy the other and does not resile from their use. As though by chance, it is always the

Enlightenment fundamentalist who oppresses and destroys the other, who can only defy it symbolically. In order to justify ourselves, we give substance to the threat by turning the *fatwa* against Salman Rushdie into a sword of Damocles hanging over the Western world, sustaining a disproportionate terror in complete misrecognition of the difference between symbolic challenge and technical aggression. In the long run, the symbolic challenge is more serious than a victorious aggression. If a simple *fatwa*, a simple death sentence can plunge the West into such depression (the vaudeville of terror on the part of writers and intellectuals on this occasion could never be portrayed cruelly enough), if the West prefers to believe in this threat, it is because it is paralysed by its own power, in which it does not believe, precisely because of its enormity (the Islamic "neurosis" would be due to the excessive tension created by the disproportion of ends; the disproportion of means from which we suffer creates by contrast a serious depression, a neurosis of powerlessness). If the West believed in its own power, it would not give a moment's thought to this threat. The most amusing aspect, however, is that the other does not believe in his powerlessness either, and he who does not believe in his powerlessness is stronger than he who does not believe in his power, be this a thousand times greater. The Arab *Book of Ruses* gives a thousand examples of this, but the West has no intelligence of such matters.

This is how we arrive at an unreal war in which the over-dimensioned technical power in turn over-evaluates the real forces of an enemy which it cannot see. And if it is astonished when it so easily triumphs this is because it knows neither how to believe in itself nor how to ruse with itself. By contrast, what it does know obscurely is that in its present form it can be anni-hilated by the least ruse.

The Americans would do well to be more astonished at their "victory," to be astonished at their force and to find an equiva-lent for it in the intelligence (of the other), lest their power play tricks with them. Thus, if the cunning but stupid Saddam had conceded one week earlier, he would have inflicted a consider-able political defeat on the Americans. But did he want to? In any case, he succeeded in his own reinstatement, whereas they had sworn to destroy him. But did they swear it? Saddam played the Americans' game at every turn, but even defeated he was the better player at ruse and diversion. The *Book of Ruses* still harbours many secrets unknown to the Pentagon.

Brecht: "This beer isn't a beer, but that is compensated for by the fact that this cigar isn't a cigar either. If this beer wasn't a beer and this cigar really was a cigar, then there would be a problem." In the same manner, this war is not a war, but this is compensated for by the fact that information is not information either. Thus everything is in order. If this war had not been a war and the images had been real images, there would have been a problem. For in that case the non-war would have appeared for what it is: a scandal. Similarly, if the war had been a real war and the information had not been information, this non-information would have appeared for what it is: a scandal. In both cases, there would have been a problem.

There is one further problem for those who believe that this war took place: how is it that a real war did not generate real images? Same problem for those who believe in the Americans' "victory": how is it that Saddam is still there as though nothing had happened?

Whereas everything becomes coherent if we suppose that, given this victory was not a victory, the defeat of Saddam was not a defeat either. Everything evens out and everything is in order: the war, the victory and the defeat are all equally unreal, equally non-existent. The same coherence in the irreality of the adversaries: the fact that the Americans *never saw* the Iraqis is compensated for by the fact that the Iraqis never fought them.

Brecht again: "As for the place not desired, there is something there and that's disorder. As for the desired place, there is nothing there and that's order."

The New World Order is made up of all these compensations and the fact that there is nothing rather than something, on the ground, on the screens, in our heads: consensus by deterrence. At the desired place (the Gulf), nothing took place, non-war. At the desired place (TV, information), nothing took place, no images, nothing but filler. Not much took place in all our heads either, and that too is in order. The fact that there was nothing at this or that desired place was harmoniously compensated for by the fact that there was nothing elsewhere either. In this manner, the global order unifies all the partial orders.

In Eastern Europe, global order was re-established in accordance with the same paradoxical dialectic: where there was something (communism, but this was precisely disorder from a global point of view), today there is nothing, but there is order. Things are in democratic order, even if they are in the worst confusion.

The Arabs: there where they should not be (immigrants), there is disorder. There where they should be (in Palestine) but are not, there is order. The fact that in the Arab world nothing is possible, not even war, and that Arabs are deterred, disappointed, powerless and neutralised, that is order. But this is harmoniously compensated for by the fact that at the marked place of power (America), there is no longer anything but a total political powerlessness.

Such is the New World Order.

A variant on Clausewitz: *non-war is the absence of politics pursued by other means* ... It no longer proceeds from a political will to dominate or from a vital impulsion or an antagonistic violence, but from the will to impose a general consensus by deterrence. This consensual violence can be as deadly as conflictual violence, but its aim is to overcome any hegemonic rivalry, even when cold and balanced by terror, as it has been over the last forty years. It was already at work in all the democracies taken one by one; it operates today on a global level which is conceived as an immense democracy governed by a homogeneous order which has as its emblem the UN and the Rights of Man. The Gulf War is the first consensual war, the first war conducted legally and globally with a view to putting an end to war and liquidating any confrontation likely to threaten the hence-

forward unified system of control. This was already the aim of
dualistic (East and West) deterrence; today we pass to the
monopolistic stage under the aegis of American power.
Logically, this democratic and consensual form should be able
to dispense with war, but it will no doubt continue to have local
and episodic need of it. The Gulf War is one of these transitive
episodes, hesitating for this reason between hard and soft
forms: virtual war or real war? But the balance is in the process
of definitively inclining in one direction, and tomorrow there
will be nothing but the virtual violence of consensus, the simul-
taneity in real time of the global consensus: this will happen
tomorrow and it will be the beginning of a world with no
tomorrow.

Electronic war no longer has any political objective strictly
speaking: it functions as a preventative electroshock against
any future conflict. Just as in modern communication there is
no longer any interlocutor, so in this electronic war there is no
longer any enemy, there is only a refractory element which
must be neutralised and consensualised. This is what the
Americans seek to do, these missionary people bearing electro-
shocks which will shepherd everybody towards democracy. It is
therefore pointless to question the political aims of this war: the
only (transpolitical) aim is to align everybody with the global
lowest common denominator, the democratic denominator
(which, in its extension, approaches ever closer to the degree
zero of politics). The lowest common multiplier being information in all its forms, which, as it extends towards infinity, also
approaches ever closer to the degree zero of its content.

In this sense, consensus as the degree zero of democracy

and information as the degree zero of opinion are in total affinity: the New World Order will be both consensual and televisual. That is indeed why the targeted bombings carefully avoided the Iraqi television antennae (which stand out like a sore thumb in the sky over Baghdad). War is no longer what it used to be ...

The crucial stake, the decisive stake in this whole affair is the consensual reduction of Islam to the global order. Not to destroy but to domesticate it, by whatever means: modernisation, even military, politicisation, nationalism, democracy, the Rights of Man, anything at all to electrocute the resistances and the symbolic challenge that Islam represents for the entire West. There is no miracle, the confrontation will last as long as this process has not reached its term; by contrast, it will stop as though of its own accord the day when this form of radical challenge has been liquidated. This was how it happened in the Vietnam war: the day when China was neutralised, when the "wild" Vietnam with its forces of liberation and revolt was replaced by a truly bureaucratic and military organisation capable of ensuring the continuation of Order, the Vietnam war stopped immediately — but ten years were necessary for this political domestication to take place (whether it took place under communism or democracy is of no importance). Same thing with the Algerian war: its end, which was believed to be impossible, took place of its own accord, not by virtue of De Gaulle's sagacity, but from the moment the maquis with their revolutionary potential were finally liquidated and an Algerian army and a bureaucracy, which had been set up in Tunisia without ever engaging in combat, were in a position to ensure the continuation of power and the exercise of order.

Our wars thus have less to do with the confrontation of warriors than with the domestication of the refractory forces on the planet, those uncontrollable elements as the police would say, to which belong not only Islam in its entirety but wild ethnic groups, minority languages etc. All that is singular and irreducible must be reduced and absorbed. This is the law of democracy and the New World Order. In this sense, the Iran-Iraq war was a successful first phase: Iraq served to liquidate the most radical form of the anti-Western challenge, even though it never defeated it.

The fact that this mercenary prowess should give rise to the present reversal and to the necessity of its own destruction is a cruel irony, but perfectly justified. We will have shamefully merited everything which happens to us. This does not excuse Iraq, which remains the objective accomplice of the West, even in the present confrontation, to the extent that the challenge of Islam, with its irreducible and dangerous alterity and symbolic challenge, has once again been channelled, subtilised and politically, militarily and religiously deflected by Saddam's undertaking. Even in the war against the West he played his role in the domestication of an Islam for which he has no use. His elimination, if it should take place, will only raise a danger-ous mortgage. The real stake, the challenge of Islam and behind it that of all the forms of culture refractory to the occi-dental world, remains intact. Nobody knows who will win. For as Hölderlin said, "where danger threatens, that which saves us from it also grows." As a result, the more the hegemony of the global consensus is reinforced, the greater the risk, or the chances, of its collapse.

The author:
Jean Baudrillard, former Professor of Sociology at the University of Paris (Nanterre), is now widely regarded as one of the most significant and controversial contemporary thinkers. His commentaries on events, objects, habits and other cultural phenomena have shaped the way global culture reflects on itself. His works in translation include *The Mirror of Production, Seduction, Fatal Strategies* and *Symbolic Exchange and Death.*

The translator:
Paul Patton lectures in Philosophy at the University of Sydney. He has previously translated essays by Baudrillard and Foucault, and recently translated *Difference and Repetition* by Gilles Deleuze. He writes on French philosophy and political theory and recently edited *Nietzsche, Feminism and Political Theory.*